PRESTON IN THE FIRST WORLD WAR

David Huggonson

AMBERLEY

First published 2014

Amberley Publishing
The Hill, Stroud
Gloucestershire, GL5 4EP

www.amberley-books.com

British Library Cataloguing in Publication Data.
A catalogue record for this book is available from the British Library.

ISBN 978 1 4456 1857 9 (paperback)
ISBN 978 1 4456 1876 0 (ebook)

Typeset in 11pt on 15pt Sabon.
Typesetting and Origination by Amberley Publishing.
Printed in the UK.

CONTENTS

ads, youre wanted:
GO AND HELP.

ACKNOWLEDGEMENTS

These names and organisations are in no particular order!

For all quotes and images taken from the *Preston Guardian*, I would like to thank Rory Brown at Briefing Media Ltd. Thanks for allowing me to also quote from the *War History of the 1st/2nd Battalion*. My gratitude to the *Lancashire Evening Post* for allowing reproduction of Cyril Cartmell's advertisement and for quoting from the *Lancashire Daily Post*. Both of these newspapers, as well as the *Preston Herald*, which is now of out print, are held by the Harris Museum (part of the Lancashire County Council). Thank you for allowing quotation from all three newspapers. Many thanks to the Lancashire Record Office for allowing quotation from the sources that they hold. My gratitude to Emma Heselwood at the Harris Museum & Art Gallery for allowing access to their sources and for permission to use them. Courtesy to the Elizabeth Roberts Archive, Centre For North-West Studies, University of Lancaster for use of their material. My gratitude goes to the Preston Grammar School Association (PGSA) and Alick Hadwen for allowing access to, and for allowing reproduction of, the content held in *The Hoghtonian* and on the PGSA website. Courtesy to the Lancashire Infantry Museum for allowing publication of the letters and photographs held in their collections. I also appreciate the permission of The Rt Hon. The Earl of Derby for permission to quote from his ancestor's letter and the Cartmell family for use of Harry Cartmell's *For Remembrance* and the portraits of Mayor and Mayoress Cartmell. Courtesy to Winter & Kidson Multimedia for use of Arthur Winter's photography and to the Tramway & Light Railway Society for allowing me to quote from J. Price's *The Dick Kerr Story* (1993).

I have written to the address of Cyril Mawbey and I have had no reply. I have also been unable to get in contact with Martin Kevill regarding Nurse de Traffords' work. Apologies for not getting permission but I have only used their work because of their contribution to this book! I am happy to discuss the use of any of these works.

My final thanks go to Aidan Turner-Bishop for his copyright advice; Andrew Walmsley for arranging the Lancashire Lantern images; Robin Utracik at Northern Studios for the *Preston Guardian* images; The Preston Digital Archive for use of its images, John Garlington for quoting from his writings and special collections and the University of Leeds for allowing a short quote of Cyril Mawbey.

Enjoy the book and I appreciate any feedback on the blog: www.preston1914.wordpress.com

All mistakes are my own.

David Huggonson
Preston
October 2013

INTRODUCTION

Some day the whole story will be told ... [1]

On the outbreak of war, Preston was a large regional centre for textiles with an active marketplace as well as a large number of shopkeepers, vendors and dealers. It was also a garrison town, with Fulwood Barracks housing the depot of the Loyal North Lancashire Regiment, the East Lancashire Regiment and the Royal Field Artillery. In 1914, Preston possessed strong travel networks north to Scotland and south to London, as well as good rail, road and canal links with Lancaster, Chorley and other north-western towns. Furthermore, Preston's large working-class population was compact and situated near the town centre, with most people employed in the town's main trades and industries, which were located there.

The town had two Conservative MPs, one of whom was George Frederick Stanley (1872–1938), who had been elected in 1910. Preston was also a passionate Roman Catholic town with a numerous local churches (H. Clemensha, *A History of Preston in Amounderness*, p. 322). It was estimated that half the population were Church of England, a third Roman Catholic, and the remainder Nonconformist (David Hunt, *A History of Preston*, p. 15). As a region Preston had a large population in the 1911 Census, which was divided by twelve ward boundaries in a comparatively compact area of 3,971 acres (both land and water):

Pre-war populations of males and females in Preston's voting wards [2]

Voting Ward	Population	Males	Females	Families/Individuals
Ashton	8,685	4,040	4,645	1,883
Avenham	7,167	2,966	4,201	1,634
Christchurch	8,418	3,967	4,451	1,884
Deepdale	10,235	4,703	5,532	2,294
Fishwick	7,366	3,304	4062	1,679
Maudland	9,355	4,440	4,915	1,999
Moorbrook	9,004	4,050	4,954	2,036
Park	14,571	6,608	7,963	3,315
Ribbleton	8,885	4,198	4,687	1,910
St John	11,727	5,537	6,190	2,543
St Peter	11,581	5,356	6,225	2,530
Trinity	10,094	4,746	5,348	2,344
Total	117,088	53,915	63,173	26,051

1

OUTBREAK OF WAR

There is one absorbing topic which occupies the minds of us all at this time and from which we cannot get away ... war.[1]

War was declared in early August 1914, and like many other towns across the country, Preston was concerned with the bank holiday and the chance for a holiday excursion. The actual news of the outbreak was reported somewhat differently in each of Preston's newspapers. *The Lancashire Daily Post*, a daily newspaper as its name suggests, published a bold, eye-catching headline on 5 August 1914: 'BRITAIN AT WAR, DECLARATION ON GERMANY LAST NIGHT'. The *Preston Herald*, a newspaper which ran every three days, published an even greater headline on 5 August 1914, certainly in scale considering its large size on the page: 'THE WAR. GERMANY INVADES BELGIUM.' The *Preston Guardian*, a weekly newspaper with a strong focus on farming, started its article on 8 August 1914 with the most flamboyant headline yet: 'WAR OF SEVEN NATIONS. GERMANS LOSE 25,000 MEN AT LIEGE.' The reason this headline contained details of casualties was because the newspaper was printed three days after the declaration of war; consequently it had more news to put into its article. The other newspapers, however, also contained details of the opening battles and their casualties. The next edition of the *Preston Herald* ran the explosive headline on 8 August 1914 of 'THE WAR. GERMAN REVERSE. BELGIANS VICTORIOUS.' The *Lancashire Daily Post* simply printed on 6 August 1914, '8,000 KILLED. GERMAN DEATH TOLL IN LIEGE.'

There was, however, a surprising absence – there was no reported large gathering of crowds in the town centre and there was no mention of people being in Preston purposefully to await news of the war. A contemporary recollected, though, that 'on that particular night on the August 4th, before war was declared, my friend and I went down to the *Preston Guardian* which is the *Lancashire Evening Post* office now and they put it on the board just after 12 o'clock that war had been declared against Germany. I remember that well.'[2] The scale of the town's subdued response to the war is clearly noticeable when compared to London, where the war was greeted very favourably and with large, enthusiastic crowds. This lack of reporting is in a complete contrast to the recollections of Harry Cartmell, Preston's mayor (1913–1919), who wrote in his autobiography, *For Remembrance*, 'During the whole of that first day, and indeed for some time afterward, great crowds of people thronged the principal streets, everyone evincing a consciousness that we were on the eve of great things.' This opinion was probably drawn from what he called an 'interesting ceremony' (p. 23). The ceremony, on 5 August 1914, was the handing over of the regimental colours, from the 1st Battalion of the Loyal North Lancashire Regiment to the mayor, before they went across to France. Cartmell quotes from the *Lancashire Daily Post* that 'considerable numbers of people lined the route, and a deep cordon of spectators, drawn up on the Market Square, followed with interest the brief ceremony which took place on the balcony [of the Harris Museum]'. Mayor Cartmell, accompanied by the town clerk and wearing his chain of office, had commented to the escort in that 'I accept these Colours of the 1st Battalion of the Loyal North Lancashire Regiment for safe custody, and will regard them as a sacred deposit until you come again in peace to reclaim them' (p. 24). The colours would be returned after the war, but at a cost. The first detachment to be sent from Preston to the front, the 1st Battalion, would, in the retreat from Mons and the engagements that followed, lose three commanding officers and a large amount of its rank and file in just a few weeks. Mayor Cartmell commented remorsefully that 'they were reduced to a mere handful' (p. 25).

* * *

It was to become quite clear that Preston's early response to the war was the mobilisation of the reservists.

> The departure from Preston of the Reservists on the night of Thursday, the 6th [August], was responsible for extraordinary scenes. Thousands of people assembled at the Depot, at Butler Street, and the Central Station. The first batch of soldiers arrived shortly before nine o'clock, and on their appearance the crowd became literally wild in their display of enthusiasm. Other detachments came in quick succession, and the station approaches were thronged until a very late hour.

Cartmell continues:

> Remarkable scenes were also witnessed outside the Fulwood Barracks on the same night. Every car was crowded with men coming in obedience to the Mobilisation Order to enrol in the Army Reserve or in the Special Reserve. The Barracks were filled to overflowing, and many of the men who had travelled long distances were in a pitiable plight. Eventually room was found for them in the Gymnasium, and the crowd gradually filtered away.
> (p. 25)

The *Preston Guardian* commented on 15 August 1914 that, as a result of such activity, 'Fulwood [became] the centre of public attraction all [that first] week'. The *Preston Herald* on 8 August 1914 added more detail under its headline 'All-Night Parade'. It explained that these 'war-smitten' crowds had formed in the rumour that a detachment

Above: Handing over of the colours, 1st Battalion Loyal North Lancashire Regiment, 5 August 1914. (Lancashire Lantern: 4914)

Left: Mayor Cartmell accepting the colours on the steps of the Town Hall. (Lancashire Lantern: 4938)

of regulars were to depart the barracks that evening. The newspaper simply commented that these rumours 'were inaccurate'. 'We used to go to the barracks,' recollected an observer, 'and watch all the battalions go away and they used to go away off time to various parts of the country.'3

'The calling up of the Territorials,' commented the mayor, 'aroused very great interest in Preston. I suppose that on the whole they were more intimately connected with the town than the Regulars, and of course, were all withdrawn at the same time from Civil Occupations ... I fear that at this stage we did not take the Territorials very seriously as a part of the combatant forces of the nation; the probabilities of Home Service work of a serious character seemed so remote' (p. 26). Despite this, the required number for the Territorial Battalion had been filled up within days. In addition, according to a report by the Lancashire *Daily Post* on 8 August 1914, a constant stream of Territorials and Regulars were reported at the post office, writing to their headquarters their intention of joining and the train details in which they would arrive. Simultaneously, Sergeant William Rawcliffe wrote in a letter home, 'There are big posters up – We want more and still more men.' Such posters were printed in local newspapers and were also placed on walls to maximise their effectiveness. Such propaganda also extended to the cinema, an often popular entertainment for locals. One such example was a series of films shown by Will Onda, a well-known entertainer and cinematographer, at the Prince's Theatre, Preston. It was reported that he was showing a series of films, many with a local theme, perhaps over the course of the week. One such film would see the departure from Preston of the 4th Battalion Loyal North Lancashire and of their movements. The *Lancashire Daily Post* added, on 22 August 1914, 'In addition, pictures of what is taking place on the actual battle ground of Europe and of the forces that are concerned therein will be features, making up a "red-hot" informative programme.' Note that the week-long showings took place the following week; see the report of the *Lancashire Daily Post* on 25 August 1914.

* * *

The topic of war was also present in Preston's Catholic churches. In the August edition of *St Thomas' Newsletter*, written 29 August 1914, the vicar begins by listing the names of acting servicemen. These men may have been either from the Territorial Army or the Regulars. The vicar also describes the view of war in a rather poetic and grand way; however, we cannot overlook how truthful these words will become as the war continued:

> There is little doubt that this will be a long and stern fight and one which will be extremely costly in life. In one way or another the whole country will feel its effects and we must prepare ourselves, if need be, to endure suffering. Our hearts will go out in deep sympathy to those who have already suffered bereavement or who will suffer in this way; this is one of the desolating features of war which we cannot avoid.

A similar view was held in *St Matthew's Magazine*. A letter was published in the August 1914 edition, likely that of the parish priest as it was his letters that seemed to be published each month.

The 4th (Territorial) Battalion Loyal North Lancashire Regiment being called up. (Lancashire Lantern: 4940)

It begins,

> My dear friends,
>   When I wrote last month's letter I said there was a fear that we were on the eve of a great European War. Our worst fears have been realised, and the biggest war this world has ever known is now waging.

The significance of this particular letter is that it shows that the subject of war had been in existence for some time. It also perhaps portrays the realisation of war for some, and perhaps also the importance of faith and of a higher power. 'Since August 10th,' writes Christopher Townson, the parish priest, 'there has been a daily service in church at 11 o'clock each morning. It has been attended by as many as 130 and as few as 30. There have been present parents, wives, sweethearts and friends of those soldiers who have left our own parish to join the Army. The object of these services is to pray that God will help us as He has helped His people in times past; and we pray that God may comfort anxious and troubled hearts.'

Similar feelings were published in the September 1914 edition of *Christ Church Magazine*. However, the unnamed author – presumably the vicar or parish priest – is able to blend together the feelings of holiday and that of the uncertainty surrounding the war – feelings that may have been felt in the wider Preston community as well as in its parishes:

> I have come to regard the Summer-holiday as providing a necessary recuperation of mind and body, without which the winter's work is sure to suffer. And there is every reason to fear that this will be exceptionally true this year … The course of the War, the safety of our sailors and soldiers, the continuance of trade and commerce, and coupled with this the securing of the necessaries of life at a price that is within the reach of all our people – these and kindred questions must be constantly in the minds of us all. To most of us this is a new experience. We felt something of it a dozen years ago during the war in South Africa, but the peril is now at our door … and none can be so dullwitted or unpatriotic as not to feel some sense of responsibility. Young and old have all a share in the task … and there must be no shirking of what each man's conscience declares to be his duty in this crisis of our Imperial destiny.

The Preston Grammar School magazine, *The Hoghtonian*, which was launched in December 1913 under strict instructions from the headmaster that it was to be produced by the boys without expecting any input or time from any member of staff, had a slightly more positive view of the war than those of the church newsletters seen above. The September 1914 editorial saw the war as a rather grand spectacle, one that would affect everyone (especially the Old Boys) and one that it wished it could contribute more to. It commented,

> We enter upon the school year at a time when our country is involved in the most momentous war in all history. It affects everyone of us as a nation, and though we at school are not yet amongst those who can answer the call to arms, much as we would wish, yet we think of the Old Boys, and we know that they have responded, and are as willing and as eager as any to be at the front. For this we honour them, and by this they preserve the regard we had for them when we were small and they were great. The School has just reason to be proud of her sons, who ever strive to uphold the motto on her doors, 'Vivat rex floreat ecclesia stet fortuna domus.' [Long live the King of the Church stands the fortune of their blooms].

With regards to the Old Boys, an attempt was made to keep a record who served. A roll of honour was published on a regular basis in *The Hoghtonian*; however, there were some difficulties in procuring the necessary details as men were often found to be excluded and constant additions had to be made.

* * *

This excitement was in complete contrast to contemporary views. In a letter addressed to Phyllis Ord by a friend on 2 August 1914, it was commented that 'I do hope this morning's paper may be mistaken and that there won't be a big European War'. Although this letter was written in Surrey, it was received in Barton, near Preston. It is just one of many letters in Colonel Rudolf Ord's large collection of wartime correspondence. The letters themselves vary in who they are addressed to but it is likely they are from family friends or from family members. Most of them are sent within England, but some are sent from the front. Unfortunately, the letters that exist are also only one side of the conversation and often reasonable assumptions have to be made. The Ord family were also well connected locally, owing perhaps to Councillor W. E. Ord, who was mayor of Preston in 1907–1908.

In a second letter, Ada Harrison, writing from Garstang on 11 August 1914 and presumably a friend of Phyllis, Rudolf's partner, attempts to console the reader at some terrible news. It begins,

11th Aug,

My dear Phyllis,
We do feel for you very much indeed and know what an anxious time you must be having. I hope you have better news of your dear one … what trouble and distress this awful war brings if not too much trouble we shall be very … [glad to hear] how Rudolf goes on. Please remember [be] … very kindly to him.

The letter continues with news of a friend's baby, an attempt perhaps to provide some gossip and news to ease someone worried about the lack of contact from her partner, especially at the outbreak of the war. The letter ends, 'I hope to hear better news of Rudolf.' A further letter from Ada hints that the situation for Rudolf might have been worse than expected:

2nd Sept [1914]

My dear Phyllis
We were very pleased to hear from your mother on Friday that your dear one is doing … as well as can be expected, his suffering must be hard to bear and to see him suffer must be awful to you but your presence will be a joy and help him to bear pain easier, we have felt most anxious to hear of him please give him our love and best wishes for a speedy recovery and we hope he will … be well enough to be removed to England … what a delight it will be to Rudolf to see his little girlie again …

Ada M Harrison

The letter again contains details of a new birth, unlikely Phyllis', but it does suggest that Rudolf had been injured and was in hospital. His injuries were not life-threatening, given the suggestion of him being moved home and the fact that Phyllis seemed to have received news of Rudolf's situation. What action he was involved and how his injuries occurred are not known. However, a later letter from Phyllis's sister in June 1915, some months after the original action, mentions the family only just having found out about an action in which the 4th Battalion had suffered high casualties. Rudolf eventually came home to England, likely to a hospital in July 1915 considering a letter he wrote on 11 July 1915. It is worth noting that previous letters put Rudolf in Surrey from July to November 1913, with the 4th Battalion, who were stationed in South Wales, which could suggest he was with his regiment at the immediate outbreak of war.

An aged Rudolf Ord. (Lancashire   A photograph of Phyllis Ord. (Lancashire Infantry Museum)
Infantry Museum)

As 1914 progressed into 1915, Ada and Rudolf decided that they would get married; whether the war, and perhaps the near loss of a loved one, was an influence remains to be seen. Separation between loved ones was also an influence on a couple getting married, especially on leave as time was usually limited for a returning soldier. Speaking of her sister's marriage, a contemporary recollected, 'They got married in December 1917 when he was home from leave. They thought the war was going to last forever and he had gone with her a long time.'[4]

* * *

Preparations to help those who would be impacted and thus suffer a great deal from the war was well under way by mid-August 1914. A Committee for the Relief of Distress was set up, and in its first meeting, on 10 August 1914, the members were printed on the very first pages of its minutes. Mayor Cartmell was chairman, and the vice-chairmen were members of other local bodies, for example the previous mayor, Mr Alderman Hayhurst. Also on the committee were clergymen; brothers John Toulmin and Sir George Toulmin of the *Preston Guardian*; Mr Hartley, later Mr Swift, of the *Preston Herald* considering the address 'Herald Office'; a chairman of a local insurance company; the presidents (and their secretaries) of local weaving and spinning trade unions; the president of the Co-Op Society; the chairman and secretary of the Trades Council; the chairman and vice-chairman of the Board of Guardians; several representatives from the Soldiers' and Sailors' Families Association; twelve local employers; the NSPCC; numerous ladies (including the mayoress and Lady Beatrix Stanley, spouse of Lord Derby) and others. The minutes of the Local Relief Committee

Sir George Toulmin of Toulmin & Sons from the *Preston Guardian*, 27 January 1923. (Courtesy of Briefing Media Ltd and Winter & Kidson Multimedia)

John Toulmin JP, brother to Sir George Toulmin, and senior member of Toulmin & Sons, from the *Preston Guardian*, 29 January 1927. (Courtesy of Briefing Media Ltd)

comment that the function of all this was 'to deal with any distress that may arise within the borough in consequence of the War, and to co-ordinate the distribution of such relief as may be required'. The money that was to be distributed came from public donations and formed part of the National Relief Fund, which had been opened by the Prince of Wales.

It was also resolved at the meeting that in order to better deal with the different parts of the borough, a subcommittee should be formed in each of Preston's voting wards. These would then work through the central committee. It was instructed that the councillors of each of these wards were to take steps to ensure that these committees would contain representation from the clergy, the town council, the board of guardians, the friendly societies, trade unions, and philanthropic societies and agencies. The next meeting of the committee took place two days later, again at the Town Hall but this time in conjunction with a meeting of ladies. Amendments were made to the committee personnel to include women, as well as representatives of other local committees and businesses. A final resolution made here was that, in the future, people would be asked whether they wished for their contribution to be made to the local fund or directly to the Prince of Wales' Fund. (CBP 53/11)

The potential of this committee was huge; within days of forming the mayor was able to announce subscriptions to the relief fund of just over £23,000. This and other details were printed in the *Preston Herald*, of 26 August 1914. However, there was some criticism of both the way the fund would be handed out and to whom it was given. An anonymous but well-educated author named 'FIAT JUSTITIA' (Let justice be done) wrote a letter to the *Lancashire Daily Post* on 19 August 1914. It was a blatant attack on the system, as the author believed people might abuse the fund after spending their wages senselessly:

> The fund ought to be administered with a liberal not to say lavish hand to the dependants of all classes of soldiers, especially of those who have gone to the front. But what of the others? What of the thriftless who, in times of booming trade, wasted their substance in riotous living? Are they to come in on equal terms with the others? ... [I]t will be a scandalous shame if the thriftless are treated as generously as the others ... I beg to suggest that an easy way of discriminating between the deserving and undeserving cases (apart from the families of soldiers) would be by forming a League of Help in Preston to be constituted by representatives of as many sections of the town as possible. Each application should be referred to the representative of that section of the town for investigation, and he [then] ... report to the committee that actually decided the matter. By this means, it would be comparatively easy to weed out the undeserving, and judiciously grade the others.

Despite this opposition, the fund was very successful. A list of names and amounts was published in the *Preston Herald* on 26 August 1914 and it illustrates that many people genuinely wanted to show that they could help, from local political unions to the local churches that had held collections especially for the fund. Some of the town's largest contributions to the fund were made by three of Preston's spinning companies: Preston Cotton Spinning & Manufacturing Co., the Cliff Spinning Co. and the Tulketh Spinning Co., each recorded as putting in £100. Unusually, the same amount was placed by a single individual, Mr William Smith, Longridge. The names of further individuals, but for lesser sums, were very common, though the amounts submitted should still be considered large, even if only £5 or £10. The generosity was even shared by the players and staff of Preston North End Football Club. Later additions were published in the *Lancashire Daily Post* on 15 August 1914 and included the very generous donation of £5,000 from Messrs Horrockses, Crewdson and Co. Ltd, and included as part of this was a further £5,000 from the directors of the company itself, each named beside the amount they donated. Sir Frank Hollins, Managing Director of Horrockses, was listed first, with his personal contribution of £1,000. There were many other individual donations from those perhaps related to serving soldiers; there was also a £100 donation from Messrs Geo Toulmin & Sons, Ltd, the publishers of the *Preston Guardian* and later Mayor Cartmell's autobiography.

In celebration, or rather perhaps in aid, of the National Relief Fund, a short piece of poetry was produced by Margaret Wilding (1899–1966) of Walton-le-Dale. The document is undated but it was likely written in late 1914 as it has a strong patriotic view and the events described in it relate to the early period in the war. Judging from its title, its primary purpose was probably to describe poetically the early events of the war in order to persuade people to contribute to the relief fund. The document also contains no price or details or a publisher, so it was possible it was not intended for general sale; it might have been a free publication or for private use. It began,

THE WAR.

Written in aid of the Relief Fund

Let us think of the heroes of bygone days, who
have won for Old England fame,
Who have died in the cause of their Fatherland,
who have helped to make England's name;
Whose noble lives of bravery we still in history read:
Who defended the honour of England's name in her
darkest hour of need.
And this bold spirit is again revived in the brave men
of to-day,
Who are so determined, at any cost, to make the
Germans pay ...

The Germans were cruel, no conscience had they,
And made up their minds to sweep Belgium away;
Was it warfare? Why no! the Germans were mad,
They would plunder, and kill, and do anything bad.
So England and France got ready to fight,
To help the oppressed and the cause of the right.

Yes, England was roused, and men with brave heart
Joined Kitchener's Army, to take a front part;
Lord Kitchener's the man we honour and treasure,
For we know well he'll give no half measure;
Yes, our soldiers are eager to make Germany yield,
And General French has command in the Field ...

Our soldiers are fighting across the wide wave,
Fighting the liberty of Europe to save,
Bearing so bravely their wounds and their pain,
To add glorious valour to Old England's name.
How is it our soldiers are honoured by all?
Because they fight bravely, and nobly they fall ...

We at home in dear England must each do our best,
To help the poor Belgians in their dire distress;
And provide for our Soldiers, who daily do fight
To defend our dear Empire, and the cause of the right.
Knowing God is our help we freely can sing,
God protect our brave Allies, and God save the King.

2

PREPARATIONS AT HOME

Preston was in a state of bustle and excitement in these early days of mobilization.[1]

In a meeting of the Preston Borough Council on 15 August 1914, several issues were resolved relating to the staffing and wages of the police in the aftermath of the outbreak of war. The council minutes show that a second issue was raised at the meeting, as fifty men were asked to be supplied from the National Reserve in order to help the police in the protection of railway lines and other vulnerable points. It was also resolved by the Finance Committee

> that the Corporation undertake that any of their Officers and Servants who are engaged in Military Service during the present War shall be re-instated on their return. That the Wages of the married Officers and Servants be paid subject to a deduction equal to the amount of the Government Pay and Allowance. That a Weekly Allowance of 5s be paid in respect of single men who have dependants.
>
> (CBP 20/37, pp. 267–268)

Similar thinking was evident at Horrockses, which posted notices in its mills stating that 'the position of every man called away by the mobilisation order will be kept open until after the war'. It continued by stating that the firm expects the wife or dependants of an employee away on active service to seek support immediately if required. A second, unnamed, firm employing 3,000 hands went further by paying 10 shillings on a weekly basis to the wife of any employee 'who, as a reservist, is called to the colours, or as a Territorial, is called up for active service'. However, this notice only applied to employees who volunteered for active service; it was printed in the *Preston Guardian* on 22 August 1914. A similar notice also appeared in the *Preston Herald* on the same date, and it showed the Lancashire & Yorkshire Railway Company also actively supporting the wives and families of its workforce, whether they were called up for service as a reservist or Territorial, whether they volunteered or even if they were called up as an ambulance man. 'Arrangements have also been made by the company for the contributions of the men to the superannuation and pension funds to be paid by the company during their absence.' The company were also to make every 'effort to find employment for the men upon their return, and, as far as possible, will reinstate them in their former position'. Dick, Kerr & Co. also provided payments to the dependants of its 260 staff who had enlisted in the early part of the war, presumably August 1914 till early 1915. The costs for this amounted to between £6,000 and £7,000 according to the details of their annual meetings. (Garraway Ltd, *History of the English Electric Company*, 1951.)

Despite such promises from employers, returning to the same job was not always viewed with gratitude. 'I was in the First World War,' commented a contemporary, 'and we were promised our jobs back [in a Bleach Works] when the war was over but the trouble was they only offered you the job you were doing before you went away. Well, you were only lads when you went away but when you came back you were twenty-three or twenty-four and they were no good were them jobs then.'[2] A second contemporary recalled that after the war, when her brother 'came out of his time there was no work so he went to Australia. He came [back] with no money, they wouldn't have him in Australia, as he had bad eyes, in the Army, so he … [went] home. But they had him here. He took my young brother, of course, my young brother was already in the Territorials.'[3]

The reason for individuals leaving places of employment to voluntarily enlist has long been debated by historians. (See Peter Simkins, *Kitchener's Army*, Pen and Sword, 1998.) One reason could have been the uncertainty of getting a wage, or even staying in a job. There was the risk that 'other lad[s who] … weren't quite old enough for the Army, they took the jobs that you would probably have had if you hadn't gone'. A contemporary, was speaking of his position as an apprentice prior to enlistment; he was going to night school, at the encouragement of his employers, to likely become a qualified bleacher with the potential to earn 30 shillings a week. He was of the opinion that he was in a fortunate position as very few learned a trade. The individual wasn't leaving for a better wage, either. He complained that 'we wasn't on a full wage when we joined the Army, really. We wasn't on a pound a week then when we joined in early 1915.'[4] Those that were self-employed or held a decent post prior to the war might have stood a chance of getting their job back. A contemporary recalled, 'Their jobs weren't guaranteed when they came out. I mean, my father being on his own as an architect, he came back to start up again. The eldest brother who was serving his articles as a solicitor, he came back [too].'[5]

Recruits, however, were not just enlisting from industry, as men were drawn from different positions, trades and backgrounds, including the local Catholic churches. *St Matthews' Magazine*, for example, states in its October 1914 edition that 'at the bottom of our church on the screen, is a list of some of the soldiers and sailors from our own parish and congregation who have joined the forces. It is a list of 80 names; and others, as we get to know them, will be added. May God defend these brave lads and men. Their cause is a just one.' Previously it had commented in its September 1914 edition that between twenty and thirty 'lads' had volunteered from its Church Lads Brigade. *St Thomas' Magazine* actually names twenty-four of those men, or lads, who were on active service from its parish in August 1914. Furthermore, *Christ Church Magazine* goes a step further in its October 1914 edition by listing the names, addresses and regiments of fifty-three parishioners. Its author explains,

I desire to give the fullest honour to those who have responded to the call of King and Country in this crisis of our history; but my chief object in printing these names is to impress upon all who see the list, and of course upon those especially who are interested because of blood-relationship, the duty of intercession in this time of anxiety. The immediate effect of the printing of the list should be to bring relations to Church at least once a week. We offer up three intercessions at three Services every Sunday, and every Wednesday evening at 7-30; and every soldier connected in any way with our church ought to have the assurance that he is represented not less than once a week in the House of God by those who are nearest and dearest to him.

It continues to do so as the war progresses and an additional eighteen, for example, were printed in November 1914. The names of those who have died was also printed alongside of those serving; the first was James Brennan, Royal Irish Regiment. However, total numbers for each of these parishes remain unknown.

Recruitment from local churches was so strong that recruits were being drawn from the teaching staff as well as the Bible classes. Furthermore, Preston's parishes were also contributing to a special battalion of the Church Lads Brigade (CLB), which would be attached to the Duke of Lancaster's Regiment. The initiative was set up similarly to the Pals Scheme, where past members, as well as current, could enlist and serve together. In fact, *St Matthew's Magazine* commented in its October 1914 edition that it had four men enlist from its CLB battalion, three of whom had become non-commissioned officers. (CLB were organised at local churches similar to modern Scout meetings, which are often held in a church hall.)

Being able to serve for the duration of the war with friends, neighbours, work colleagues, and even family was also a strong reason to enlist. A good example of this was in the formation of the Preston Pals, also known as D Company, 7th Battalion, Loyal North Lancashire Regiment. It began with the publication of an appeal in the *Lancashire Daily Post* from 31 August to 2 September 1914. It read,

It is proposed to form a Company of young business men, clerks etc., to be drawn from Preston and the surrounding districts and to be attached, if practicable, to a Battalion of the Loyal North Lancashire Regiment. Will those who would like to join apply here any afternoon or evening this week – the earlier the better. Cyril Cartmell, Town Hall, Preston.

The author of the newspaper appeal was Cyril Cartmell, the son of the mayor, Harry Cartmell, and its success was remarkable. 'So satisfactory was the response,' wrote Mayor Cartmell, 'that on the Thursday afternoon [the appeal began on the Monday] Major Faulder was informed that the Company was assured. On the Sunday morning the 250 men thus got together were medically examined at the Public Hall, and it is noteworthy, in contrast to the usual state of things, that there were only five or six rejections on physical grounds' (p. 36).

Word of mouth was also an effective method of recruitment, as Cyril Mawbey recollected:

At the end of August 1914 after a few white feathers I cycled over to Preston, one of my friends having told me he had signed on with the Preston Pals. I was too late for the first contingent and was the first name down for the second 250. My friend phoned to say a few had failed to turn up so I got the next train to Preston and tagged along with the procession on its way to the station and Tidworth ... That phone call saved me from Lancs. Fusiliers & Gallipoli.

(p. 18)

Mayor Cartmell adds, 'On the Monday the men were attested at the Guild Hall and at midnight fell into line in the Market Square and marched to the Station amid cordial manifestations of approval and goodwill on the part of a vast crowd of people' (p. 36). They later departed for their training camp at Tidworth where they would forge a reputation, one that was to be enhanced on the battlefield. For a history of the Preston Pals, see my blog – the website address is at the front of the book.

* * *

The timing of the Preston Pals advertisement coincided with the town's larger voluntary recruitment boom. The size of the Preston Pals – which was only a company of 250 men – would become only a shadow to the bigger rush to the colours. Actual figures are not available but suggested figures are in the thousands. It was reported that ever since the call to arms 'the business of recruitment has been abnormally active, but it was not until last weekend that the prevailing boom set in'. The report in the *Preston Guardian* on 5 September 1914 continued, 'On Saturday last [29 August] so many recruits arrived that the recruiting staff was not equal to the task of enrolling them all, and many had to go away till Monday.' The *Lancashire Daily Post* on 31 August 1914 reported that recruiting by this point for the 'first Kitchener battalions has been completed, and a good start made with the Kitchener battalions'. Recruitment, however, was also taking place into other branches, such as the artillery and the cavalry, as well as the infantry. On 5 September 1914, the *Preston Guardian* also printed,

Both the Loyal North Lancashire and East Lancashire Regiments have practically completed the enrolment of two new Kitchener battalions, and are recruiting steadily for a third. The second Kitchener battalions were filled up in less than four days. The R.F.A. [Royal Field Artillery] have been still more fortunate, recruits of a splendid type having come up in such numbers that over 6,000 have been enrolled, many of them being sent to the training camps.

If each battalion was approximately 1,000 men, and we do not include those battalions still recruiting, the number of men recruited by early September was at least 10,000. These figures, however, cannot be relied upon because we do not know where the newspaper report got its information, or whether it was accurate. In addition, the reported figures might have been exaggerated. Peter Simkins points out that by '12

RECRUITING.

It is proposed to form a Company of Young Business Men, Clerks, &c., to be drawn from Preston and the Surrounding Districts, and to be Attached, if practicable, to a Battalion of the Loyal North Lancashires.

Will those who would like to join apply here any Afternoon or Evening this week—the Earlier the Better.

CYRIL CARTMELL.

TOWN HALL, PRESTON,
Aug. 31st, 1914.

Cyril Cartmell's advertisement in *The Lancashire Daily Post*, printed in August and September 1914. (*Lancashire Evening Post*)

Cyril Cartmell in uniform. (Courtesy of the Cartmell Family)

Cyril with fellow Pals at Tidworth. (Courtesy of the Cartmell Family)

The Preston Pals assemble on the Market Square, 7 September 1914. (Lancashire Lantern: 4941)

September 1914, 478,893 men had joined the Army, 301,971 having enlisted in the fortnight after 30 August' (p. 75). For Preston to recruit even a small fraction is rather impressive but whether it did remains debatable.

The sudden rush of recruits into a town that was already struggling for space presented many problems, the largest of which was accommodation at the barracks, which only had room for around 1,000 recruits; with double that number arriving each day, it was no surprise that these living quarters were, according to the *Preston Guardian* on 5 September 1914, 'taxed to the utmost'. Such a rush was expected at the barracks, even before August 1914. Mr Dennis, who had grown up in and lived in military housing, recalled that 'sometime before August 1914 one and all had to move out of the barracks, married quarters were needed for the intake of recruits. I remember many horse-drawn furniture vans coming to move soldiers' families ... Mother, my sisters, and self followed in the wake of our van from the barracks, I think I did get a ride on Mary's pram when I was tired. We moved into this requisitioned house and I remember a hole in the floor and being told to keep away from it as the floor was rotten ... This property ... [was later] pulled down under slum clearance.'[6]

'At that time they were sleeping anywhere, in the parks,' commented a contemporary, 'as there was no room at the barracks for them, it was packed. People went around taking them in their houses for somewhere to sleep and mother was one. She brought these two lads in. They were at our house until they went away. They used to go to the barracks every day and as soon as there was enough for a battalion, they were off ... They wrote to mother to thank her, Arthur and the other boy.' Those men that stayed with the Preston family had travelled from Liverpool to enlist voluntarily at Preston, and it was also how the author of the comment met her husband. This was not a one off: 'We had quite a few [soldiers] coming and going ... from the barracks ... They used to ask if they could bring their wives to stay. I made quite a lot of nice friends, we never had anybody objectionable.'[7]

Another solution to the problem of housing was the erection of tents and marquees 'on the recreation grounds adjoining the barracks, and ... it was decided early in the week to send detachments [averaging over 2,000 per day] to the training stations without waiting for uniform and accoutrements'. In addition, the situation was aided by the Public Hall, Fulwood Workhouse and other public buildings being utilised for temporary shelter in mid-September, according to the *Preston Guardian*. Mayor Cartmell adds that 'men were [also] welcomed as guests ... in Schools [and] Clubs ... entertainments were improvised, and hot-pot suppers provided' (p. 32). He continues,

> The Tramway power station opened its doors nightly for a reception of 500 soldiers. With a plentiful supply of hay the lofts were regarded as luxurious sleeping quarters. What happened at the power station was rather typical than exceptional. At a moderate computation, some 3,000 soldiers must in this way have enjoyed the hospitality of our townsmen during this trying period of congestion at the barracks.
>
> (p. 32)

However, not all were happy with the arrangements; 250 miners from Tonypandy, South Wales, had marched to Preston railway station in protest with a banner reading, 'No Food, no Shelter, no Money.' They had given up everything to serve their country. They had left their wives at home and had no money to send to them. They would not go back to the barracks unless their pay was secured (pp. 32–34). A contemporary recalls, 'I remember ... all them lads from Wales and people running with food for them and feeding them on the flag market.'[8] It was later arranged they would be paid the following day, but at a cost. Mayor Cartmell, the town clerk and Sir George Toulmin (MP for Bury, managing director of the *Lancashire Daily Post* and the *Preston Guardian*) were to witness first-hand the struggles that recruitment staff were facing at Fulwood Barracks. 'Every effort was being made to keep pace with the demands put on them. The adjutant said that on the previous night he had remained at his desk till 3 o'clock, and would have gone on longer if one of his clerks had not fallen off his stool in a swoon' (p. 34).

A letter expressing thanks as well as a poem was printed in the *Preston Herald* on 19 September 1914.

* * *

Applications for recruitment during August – just prior to the rush – were taking place at specially made recruiting offices at the New Infants' School in Watling Street Road, Fulwood, as well as at No. 8 Nile Street (near Derby Street); both had been requisitioned. According to the *Lancashire Daily Post*, on 7 August and 8 August 1914 the Fulwood and Cadley schools in Victoria Road were also taken over to sleep troops. However, once the reservists of the East Lancashire, the Loyal North Lancashire and the RFA had been mobilised the use of the Fulwood schools was no longer needed. Eventually, on 10 August it was reported that there was more space available at barracks 'for the housing and training of recruits in comfort.' Recruits could still apply locally to 'Sergeant Livesey, 8, Nile Street, or Colour-Sergeant Higginson, 7, Taylor-street, Fulwood [off Broadgate, Penwortham].' (As part of the process, recruits received pay from the time of enlistment until the attestation process was completed, when they were handed over to the depot staff and housed in the barracks for drill and equipment training under Army conditions. The Loyal North Lancashire Regiment's recruitment stations were on the right of the square, the left – as well as those in the regimental depot located in the barracks – being those of the East Lancashire Regiment.) A contemporary recalls from childhood that 'trams used to be going up here and we used to come to the door and see that they were going up again and we used to go up and see all the soldiers' faces pressed against the cars. I [also] remember once seeing this chap frogmarched all the way from the railway station to Fulwood Barracks. I don't know what he had done, probably a deserter.'[9] The trams used to run from the barracks all the way to the railway station, ideal for the movement of troops.

The rush to enlist did not last long; by 19 September 1914, the *Preston Guardian* had reported that Fulwood Barracks was managing to cope with the rush and was now dispatching large drafts of men to the various military training centres to ease its accommodation problems. This, however, was not the concern.

> The number of recruits arriving from day to day has been somewhat smaller, partly on accounts of the order under which they were posted to the Reserves and sent home to be called for, and partly on account of the raising of the standard as to height and chest measurement. The reserve order was suspended earlier this week, however, and all men offering themselves were accepted at once for immediate training … The effects of these changed conditions will bring recruits to the depots in greater numbers during the next few days.

This may have been the case in the short term but, following an absence of recruitment news, the *Preston Guardian* reported on 14 November 1914 that recruiting numbers were now just 'brisk'.

The recruitment strategies that followed were designed to increase recruitment; they were devised by the Parliamentary Recruitment Committee. One such strategy was rather radical and it was suggested by a letter writer in the *Preston Herald*, 12 September 1914. He suggested that every unmarried man aged between eighteen and forty-two entering any football ground should be presented with the coward's badge – the white feather.

The first workable idea, however, was publicly held meetings, the first example of which was held in Preston's Public Hall. It was attended, quite significantly, in person by Lord Derby, a title given to those of a powerful North West family that held large estates of which Preston was a part. Lord Derby was a well-connected individual both politically and

A tram posing with its banners and recruitment slogans in early 1915. (Preston Digital Archive)

socially in the North West and was infamous for his wartime recruitment speeches. (See Peter Simkins, *Kitchener's Army*.) In attendance at the meeting were the mayor, the town clerk, several magistrates and military representatives. The *Preston Guardian* reported on 28 November 1914 that, in order to advertise and maximise the possible attendance, a boldly printed appeal on a large placard was created, reading, 'This gallant [L. N. L.] regiment wants recruits. Will all who are willing to join come and meet Lord Derby at the Public Hall, Preston tonight.' The talk concluded with an emotional appeal:

> I have got a cold, and am not going to pretend to make a long speech. I am only making an appeal to you personally as a town with which my family has been most intimately connected, and I hope always will be. I want to feel proud of Preston, and that Preston is justified in its name 'Proud Preston', and that can be done if you really make a response to the appeal which not I, not any of the writers in the press, but the men who are fighting our battles in the trenches are making. They are the people who are appealing to you.

This strategy continued into 1915, not in the town centre but in the smaller communities outside Preston. The reporting in the *Preston Guardian* from November 1914 to January 1915 contains brief mentions of small recruitment meetings. However, there were other attempts to persuade local men to enlist. On 17 May 1915, the *Lancashire Daily Post* reported,

Below left: An anxious new recruit expresses his willingness to enlist. (Courtesy to Briefing Media Ltd)

Below right: In Preston the trams were able to take troops from the train station to Fulwood Barracks and the other way around. (Preston Digital Archive)

A great recruiting campaign, inaugurated by the West Lancashire Territorial Association [with Lord Derby as its Chairman], was opened at Preston, this morning [Monday, 17 May 1915], when Lord Derby's Band of 65 skilled instrumentalists and pipers of the Liverpool Scottish arrived in town at 9.30 from Bolton. They were met by the police and ... [escorted] to billets for their stay in Preston.

The whirlwind campaign in Preston is part of a scheme to cover the whole of the West Lancashire, the aim of which is to enrol immediately at least 8,000 Territorials in the reserve units of the West Lancashire Division in order to repair the wastage of the men now on active service. There are, at the present time, no fewer than 12,000 West Lancashire territorials serving at the front, and one of the objects of the campaign is to bring home to the people how magnificently their own lads from home have [shown] ... their valour and worth in some of the toughest fighting ever known ...

The campaign opened at noon to-day, the bands and speakers assembling at the Town Hall and following a route through Friargate, Adelphi-street, Trafford-street, Brackenbury-road, Ripon-street, Garstang-road, and Lancaster-road, halting at intervals for brief stirring appeals to the crowds.

This campaign continued into the week and the highlight was a second speech by Lord Derby, who was a strong believer in voluntary recruitment, to a large crowd of Prestonians on the market square. The *Preston Guardian* reported the significance of the visit:

With the probable exception of the visit of the King and Queen two years ago [in 1913], there has been no more impressive scenes in Preston market square than that witnessed on Wednesday night, when Lord Derby addressed a great recruiting meeting, and rounded off the campaign which had been in progress during the week. There must have been a crowd of at least 20,000, who were entertained during the period of waiting by the massed band of 140 instrumentalists, and the pipers of the Liverpool Scottish who were grouped on the balcony in front of the Free Library.

When Lord Derby and the mayor (Alderman Cartmell) appeared on the steps of the Town Hall a great cheer was raised. Accompanying his lordship ... [among Officers with important local positions] ... Captain A. M. Hollins [who raised 'Hollins Company'], Sir F[rank] Hollins [his father and Managing Director of Horrockses] ... and other prominent local employers.

The mayor, after making a strong appeal on behalf of the different units, said that he hoped in Captain Hollins' company would be found many from the cotton mills. Men could not be spared from many of the mills without inconvenience, but they had all got to suffer inconvenience just now. At the beginning of the war they used the motto, 'Business as usual.' There was now only one business that mattered, and that was to get rid of the enemy. The business of all according to their individual capacity was to take a hand in bringing the criminal to justice. (Applause.)

Lord Derby spoke on two things that were keeping back a number of men. Some said, 'We won't go till we are fetched.' Well, Lord Kitchener wanted 300,000 men, and if he did not get them one way he would get them another. They did not want it to be said of

Lord Derby's recruitment speech is heard by the Preston public – May 1915. (Lancashire Lantern: 4947)

Lord Derby's Liverpool Band play to the crowd – May 1915. (Lancashire Lantern: 4948)

This float was part of a similar procession, which took place in October 1915 to raise funds for the provision of winter comforts for the troops on the front. *Preston Guardian*, 9 October 1915. (Courtesy of Briefing Media Ltd)

Preston, or any other Lancashire town, that when men were called upon to help their brother townsmen fighting at the front, they had to be fetched.

Another thing, and one with which he had great sympathy, was the reluctance of mothers to let their sons go to the front. 'I know what their feelings are,' he continued, 'because I have got my own son fighting in the trenches at this moment. If I had kept my son from doing what he clearly recognised to be his duty, he would at the end of the war be pointed out as a man who knew his duty but failed to do it. Mothers and fathers, let me say this to you, if you keep him for the moment, you are going to make him lose his own self-respect, and when the war is over you will find that when he has lost his self-respect he will equally have lost his affection for you who prevented him from doing his duty.'

'I ask you to read the story of what went on in Belgium, the story of the *Lusitania*, of the poisonous gases in France, and the poisoned wells in South Africa, and when you have read it you can't be human if you don't let your sons go to fight for this country, to prevent such things ever happening here and to avenge the women and children whom these brutal Huns have murdered, both in the sea to the south of Ireland and in Belgium across the water.' (Cheers.)

'It is difficult,' continued Lord Derby, 'to speak at an open-air meeting, and difficult, perhaps, to make you understand all that I feel; but if you could only understand one part of what I feel, there is not a young man – and I am only appealing to-night to the young men – who won't come forward and say, 'I will do my duty. I won't go looting shops and breaking heads of Germans in England, but I will put my hate to the purpose it ought to be put to – fight the enemy in the field and subjugate him once and for all.' (Cheers.)

Lord Derby concluded his brief speech by appealing for a large influx of recruits for the Territorial or Regular battalions of the Loyal North Lancashire Regiment, which had a glorious past and even more glorious future. (Cheers.)

On 20 May 1915, the *Lancashire Daily Post* reported the response to Lord Derby's speech under the headline 'RUSH OF RECRUITS. Splendid Response at Preston. Enthusiasm follows Lord Derby's Appeal'. It continues,

The rush of recruits after last night's big demonstration at Preston was so great that the available staffs were not able to deal with them, although the recruiting stations were kept open until 10.30, and in some instances later.

Definite figures are not yet available, but at least 150 men joined the various units. This morning the various units were busily engaged in attesting and examining recruits.

The recruits in the present campaign up to this morning are as follows:

2nd West Lancs. RFA   155
4th L.N.L. (Reserve) Batt.   90
Capt. A. M. Hollins' Company 115

These figures do not include the impetus given to recruiting in the regular line regiments, or those which have joined the 4th Battalion Royal Lancasters, at the Fishergate recruiting office, or the Liverpool Scottish, so that, in round figures at least 400 men have joined since the campaign opened … The need for a big influx of recruits to this reserve battalion [4th Loyal North Lancashire] is so great that a staff of seven Preston officers has been especially sent down from Oxted to continue the campaign. These officers are practically all connected with the great cotton firms in the town, and their very names are a guarantee to all cotton operatives joining the ranks of steady employment after the war. A recruiting office for the 4th L[oyal]. N[orth]. L[ancashire]. is to be opened in Church-street shortly, and we are informed that a large supply of uniforms arrived yesterday, so that new recruits are put into khaki as soon as they pass the doctor ...

* * *

The recruitment for Hollins' company, much like Cyril Cartmell had done with the Preston Pals, was helped, or at least publicised, by a daily advertisement in the *Lancashire Daily Post* from 18 to 29 May. It read,

Join The Special Company of the 11th Batt[alion]. LOYAL NORTH LANCS. which is being raised by Capt. A. M. Hollins. Immediate Uniform. Join your Townsman and train with him at Chichester. Give in Your Name at TOWN HALL or PUBLIC HALL. Preston Lads For a Preston Regiment.

This advertisement took a brief break but returned two days later – one was a Sunday – with the following on 1 June 1915:

CAPT. A. M. HOLLINS is open to accept 50 MORE MEN of Good Character & Physique for his Special Company. Come at Once.

The small print read,

A Doctor will be in attendance at the Public Hall from 7 to 9 p.m. on Tuesday and Wednesday for the purpose of examining recruits.
   The Company will Leave Preston on Thursday Next leaving barracks 8.30 p.m., and will halt in the Market place.

This advertisement appeared alongside other advertisements that related to Lord Derby's Territorial recruitment campaign:

Wanted! 1,000 MEN For The 4th Loyal North Lancashire Regiment. Join The Old Preston Territorial Battalion Now At The Front. Local Officers. Local Men. Apply: Town Hall, or Avenham Lane Drill Hall, Preston. God Save The King.

It appeared around the same period as Hollins' advertisement but it was not as consistent. However, there was some concern about what would be called 'Hollins' Company'. In a letter to Sir George Arthur on 5 July 1915, Lord Derby wrote that

Captain Hollins, a very well known local man ... tells me that during the last ten days he has been round trying to get men for his special company in the Regulars. He has got altogether twenty-five and he had answers from five hundred or six hundred to the effect that they would only come when they were fetched ... I confess it makes one despair as to the result of the war.

The date of the above letter does create confusion as the company was recruited in May, and, according to the advertisements, left in the same month for training at Chichester. The connection between Lord Derby and Sir Frank Hollins could be explained perhaps through politics. While Sir Hollins was chairman of the Preston Liberal Association, Lord Derby's brother, George Frederick Stanley, was Conservative MP for Preston 1915–1918. Perhaps more likely was an association through their powerful family titles; Sir Hollins was given the title Baronet of Greyfriars in the parish of Broughton, Lancaster, on 29 November 1907.

* * *

Recruitment for the Regulars may have been slow but not for the Territorials, as seen above, or the Artillery. '[From] this time onward,' writes Mayor Cartmell, 'no difficulty was ever experienced in filling the ranks of the Artillery. Altogether it was estimated that 1,000 men were secured by this rally'(p. 40). Despite the success, no improvement was made with regards to recruiting into the Army. It was clear the town needed something to maximise and promote enlistment, with as much pageantry, style and effort as possible. This it was to receive, and again the driving force was Lord Derby. A garden fête was organised on his instruction and was held in Avenham and Miller parks on 26 August 1915 on behalf of the 4th (Territorial) Battalion Loyal North Lancashire Regiment. Despite being unable to attend in person, Lord Derby's fête was attended by thousands, according to the *Preston Guardian*. The fête was also part of a week-long recruitment campaign that saw key local speakers conducting meetings in every suitable spot in the town and district, as well as parades and a moving-picture van visiting the outskirts of the town each night. 'I recall [as a child] what must have been a recruiting campaign, a military band paraded through the town with many men following, some carrying slogans. I also "fell in" and eventually finished up at the police station lost. I was in due course claimed by my mum but could not see why I could not be, like my dad, a soldier.'[10] Unfortunately, once again, the response at the regimental depots was not as expected. Similar feelings were echoed in a letter dated 23 August 1915 from Rudolf Ord, who was recuperating at Weeton Camp, near Kirkham, in which he commented, 'I may go into Preston tomorrow [to] this recruiting meeting. But as I am an Orderly Officer it may fall through.' This reference, however, is hard to interpret as it could mean that his involvement in the event, and not the meeting itself, may have fallen through.

In response a further recruitment strategy was started, one that was designed to maximise voluntary recruitment as conscription was not seen as the ideal solution, even though it was looming. Firstly, a census took place to establish how many men between the ages of fifteen and sixty-five were working in each trade; this was part

A portrait of Sir Frank Hollins by Frank O'Sailsbury. (Courtesy of the Harris Museum and Art Gallery, Preston)

The Garden Fête at Miller Park from *Preston Guardian*, 28 August 1915. (Courtesy of Briefing Media Ltd)

of the National Registration Act enacted in July 1915. The details of this census were formed into a national register. The work of the census took much organising, as a meeting in July 1915 of the Finance Committee of Preston Council showed. It was agreed that 300 docket envelopes at a cost of 30 shillings per hundred would be purchased for the purpose of containing the registration forms for each enumerator. (CBP/28/8, p. 322)

However, this new strategy was seen by Mayor Cartmell as the 'first step in the direction of compulsory military service', although this view does not seem to have registered with the local community. (p. 43) The town was still attempting to stimulate recruitment through local means and, much like other recruitment schemes during 1915, was still apparently being met by a strong response from the community. Evidence of this is witnessed in the coverage of the *Preston Guardian* in early October 1915.

However, not long after Derby took up his position as Director of Recruiting on 11 October 1915, he became chairman of the Parliamentary Recruitment Committee. One of his first ideas was that in every Parliamentary area a canvass would be worked with the intensity of a Parliamentary election. On 21 October 1915, Lord Derby announced what would become known as the grouping scheme or the Derby Scheme. This strategy was widely regarded as a desperate last attempt to preserve the voluntary system, or as a necessary prelude to the introduction of conscription. The scheme did not apply to Ireland, but elsewhere a personal canvass of every man between the ages of eighteen and forty-one was carried out on the basis of the national register. Each man was asked either to join up immediately or attest his willingness to serve when summoned. The attested men would be separated into two categories, single and married, each then subdivided into twenty-three groups according to age. Groups would be called up in strict order as and when required, beginning with single men of nineteen. The youngest married men would not be called up until all twenty-three age groups of single men had been called up. The canvassing was completed in Preston on the evening of 5 November – ahead of the 30 November 1915 deadline. The *Preston Guardian* advised on 4 December 1915 that men could offer themselves for attestation immediately, before their groups were called, and that they could do so at the 'Public Hall, Stanley Street Artillery Depot, or at the Avenham Lane L[oyal]. N[orth]. L[ancashire]. Territorial Depot. Any queries were to be passed onto the Preston Recruitment Committee or the Harris Free Library.'

The organisation of the recruits during Lord Derby's Grouping Scheme was far more organised than it was during the August 1914 rush. It had to be as the town was to serve two regimental districts, the first from the 47th (Preston, Bolton, Horwich, Chorley and Kirkham) and the second from the 38th (Burnley, Blackburn, Accrington, Nelson, Colne, Darwen, Haslington, Bacup and adjoining townships). Those from the 47th would be sent to the Public Hall and those from the 38th were sent to Fulwood Barracks. 'The calls [of the groups] were so arranged that from each district some 150 men to 200 men should report themselves, so that there should be no congestion,' reported the *Preston Guardian* in January 1916. 'At each centre a medical board of five Army doctors sat to examine the men, and to set aside those not considered fit for general field service, to be allotted to garrison duty or departmental work. The necessary documents enrolling each man in his future regiment or other unit were then completed, and the men were sent to the barracks pending their dispatch to the depot of their regiment.' The report concluded that these 'systematic arrangements [were] found to work smoothly and well'. This not only illustrates Preston as a recruitment hub but shows that the previous system of men walking into a depot to enlist was not longer usable; in addition, a system where men were accommodated in large numbers at Fulwood Barracks also seems to have been abandoned.

However, there were two serious problems with the Lord Derby's Grouping Scheme. The first was that the overall figures, published by the *Preston Guardian* on 16 January 1916, showed that single men had held back from enlistment and that married men, who had been told they would be called up last, had attested in larger numbers than single men. Lord Derby's report on his recruitment campaign was published in January 1916. The figures revealed that of the 2,179,231 bachelors that the national register showed were available, 1,029,231, or nearly half, had not attested. Those unaccounted for included the 651,160 single men not in starred or protected occupations deemed important to the war effort. Through a careful deduction of this number, by removing the possible exemptions and rejections that the tribunals may pass, it was estimated that the scheme had produced only 343,386 single men. Preston's figures were different as positive results were obtained through its canvassing work and there was a strong indication that the town may have been patriotic.

The *Preston Guardian* on 16 January 1916 explained that the town had a total figure of 13,500 eligible men according to the national register, of which 898 had already enlisted, while 8,884 had attested under the Derby Scheme. Within the total figure, 5,400 were single men and 8,100 were married. A second comparison can be made with the national pattern, as Preston also had a large number of men who had not attested. Among the total of 2,390 unattested it was estimated that 1,000 men had failed to give an adequate reason. The report suggested 'that many may have since joined the forces, or come into the Reserves during the past week'.

The first Military Service Bill, which established the principle of conscription, was placed before Parliament on 5 January 1916. When it received royal assent on 27 January, it was to specifically apply to unmarried men and widowers without children or dependants between the ages of eighteen and forty-one. It exempted those who were involved with important war work, the sole supporters of dependants, the unfit and approved conscientious objectors. The Act also gave statutory authority to the tribunals that were set up under the Derby Scheme. These tribunals were the second serious problem with Lord Derby's scheme, as they would have a serious impact on Preston's workers and their families, as the next chapter will show. Things were not helped by the introduction of the Defence of the Realm Act in 1914, which among many things granted the government the power to take over any land or company, as well as being able to censor newspapers.

SINGLE MEN

Hundreds of Thousands of married men have left their homes to fight for **KING & COUNTRY**

SHOW YOUR APPRECIATION

BY FOLLOWING THEIR NOBLE EXAMPLE

3

WORK OF WAR

I was in the Army in the First World War, I was conscripted. Things in those days were hard for working people. If you were poor it was almost criminal, your own fault, laziness. Yet when you went for work you got next to nowt for it, the bosses got the money.[1]

The war was requiring more men; local industries and companies were losing valuable manpower. Preston was no exception; there is evidence of men being lost, or recruited from its local companies. For example, at Horrockses, or perhaps one of its subsidiary businesses, between May and July its fourteen-strong workforce had been reduced, even if only by one or two men. By October 1915, the lost labour had been replaced – and even increased – by women, but only on a day-to-day basis. The working female population would grow, and would remain part of the overall workforce long after the end of the war, into the 1920s. (DDHS 39)

***

A contemporary who was trained by her brother before he left to enlist stated, 'I did all the paraphernalia [including the bookkeeping]. In those days it was a wholesale kind of thing because the wagons went from the colliery [she worked for a coal merchant] to the various places and we had to make out the vouchers and things. I was [by] myself for a long time and I had one or two funny affairs with men that came and wouldn't go away so I got another girl to help me.' This was not just a one-off; 'the [Fulwood] barracks, they [also] used a lot of army pay-girls during the war'.[2] Young boys, as well as girls, had to take on additional duties: 'When father was called up, my eldest brother went and my baby brother had to start work doing something. He was more or less waiting to be called-up. So I was in charge at about twelve in the house.'[3]

The war did not just provide opportunities for employment, it also allowed women to get a better wage: 'I got 2/-d a week [for dressmaking] … I started at 10/-d a week in the 1914 war and when I left I was getting about 18/-d and that was marvellous.'[4] The war effort also provided opportunities for bringing work away from the factory floor and into the home, but this was not always done by choice. Mr Dennis's mother, for example, was sewing soldiers' shirts for 6*d* each; she managed to do eighty in a week. This had occurred because, after volunteering for active service, his father's 'records were lost and mother got no allowance for six months'.[5] However, there were benefits to working from home instead of in the mills: 'My eldest sister was a great help … [and] by working at home she was in contact with her children and during school holidays and Saturdays … '

The war would also affect those women who were already working in the cotton industry. Helen recollected the impact of the war on her working hours: 'I know we used to work on a Saturday morning till 12 o'clock, and then during the war we used to start at 6 o'clock till 8 o'clock. I used to go home at 8 o'clock for my breakfast and back at half past eight and then till half past five … making parachutes.' Prior to the war, when she first started, aged fourteen, she worked 'half-past seven till half-past five. We had an hour for dinner. We worked long hours … It weren't a big wage … [And it] used to vary. If your looms were stopped you didn't get as much. If they were stopped for anything else your money was stopped.' The wages would vary week to week, 'anything from £2 to £4. Sometimes we might wait on beams during the wartime. They closed one shed during the war and they just had the other two. In one shed they would sew the sheets.'[6] One lady, who had also worked in the cotton industry as a child, had contrasting experiences: 'I loved working in the mill and I loved weaving … It was noisy and all that but I got used to it. I was interested! They used to say that I was a good weaver. During the war I was friendly with a girl and we used to go out together. Sometimes we would go out and then we would talk about it the day after.'[7] A further contemporary recalled: 'My other sister. She was up at the barracks [working in records]. She gave her job up and then she played football in those early days with the team from Fulwood Barracks … There wasn't alot [of ladies' football] but there was Dick, Kerr's Ladies, a local team and a wonderful team too … They [Fulwood Barracks] made a team up from records … [None came from mills as they were usually too tired.] It was a new thing but people used to enjoy it and there were never any complaints about it.'[8]

* * *

Preston's recruitment problems were not limited to its cotton industry; they also affected its smaller industries, for example Harding Coach Makers. Its account book illustrates the effect of recruitment on its workforce. For the week ending 6 August 1914, the company paid a total of sixty-eight men. The crafts and responsibilities varied, from clerks to coach builders; the company were also training apprentices and employed individuals performing single tasks, for example wheelwrights. The average wage was 9½*s* for a day's work, Monday to Friday; however, this amount increased or decreased depending on the responsibility and skill level of the worker's position (DDX 460/19, pp. 79–80). It was noted that twenty-three of Harding's workers had 'territorial job' written by their name in the margin in the second week of August 1914 (pp. 81–82). The previous chapter has already shown that these early days saw the Territorial Army mobilised; only one member of staff was lost, though, and that

A woman pouring gunpowder into an artillery shell. (Lancashire Lantern: 4953)

wasn't until the following week (pp. 83–84). The workforce numbers would stay consistent and the wages would too until 7 September 1914, when short time was introduced and workers were paid less than they had for a full day's work the week before; everyone, including the foreman, took a pay cut, working for 7½s; only the clerks were unaffected in their £1 daily salary (p. 100). Soon after this – the exact date is not known – W. Rainey, a labourer, would 'enlist in K[itchener's] Army'; his recent drop in wage, from 9½s to 5½s, may have been a key factor in him enlisting (p. 101). By January 1915, five more men had left. Three had enlisted – one in the 'L. N. L Regt' (p. 110), one as a Territorial (p. 148) and another as an Army clerk (p. 137) – and two had their pay stopped (pp. 119, 121), although this could have been related to injury (p. 125). The New Year also seemed to bring a wage rise for some, although workers were still being lost, either for no reason or due to enlistment (pp. 169, 173). There was little improvement by September 1915, as more men had enlisted – six were lost in June 1915 alone (pp. 252, 254). Men were even leaving for other companies, such as Dick, Kerr & Co., to work on munitions or shell making; they were also leaving for no reason. By 5 August 1915, almost a year since the outbreak of war, the company was down to fifty-two workers from an original sixty-eight – a loss of sixteen men, most of whom were lost to the war (p. 285). The records do not show whether women were employed to replace the lost workforce. Some pencil notations at the rear of the account book indicate that five men (including Rainey) were lost in August and September 1914 (p. 294).

A similar pattern was witnessed in Preston's agricultural district as large numbers of farms in the Fylde area experienced a shortage of workers as many left the fields either to enlist or because they were called up as reservists. However, it was only in the last week of August 1914, according to the *Preston Guardian* on 5 September 1914, that 'rural districts [began to hold] public meetings [which] were organised by civic and urban authorities at which large numbers of men joined, afterwards marching to Fulwood [Barracks] in compact bodies'. Concern for this was expressed by the Preston branch of the Lancashire Agricultural War Committee. It complained that 'in the opinion of this Committee there is already an insufficient supply of labour … [we] protest most strongly against the withdrawal of any more labour from the land, and urge the War Agricultural Committee to do all in its power to prevent such withdrawal'.

This concern was expressed in early 1916, but the reported shortage of labour in the Preston was not yet acute; it would not become serious until the spring (WAM/1, pp. 50–52). However, solutions were being put forward to these local committees, usually in the form of questionnaires. One had asked, providing suitable arrangements could be made, if farmers would avail themselves of their labour for recruitment in exchange for female workers. The Preston Branch responded somewhat favourably to the idea, but only providing the arrangements were indeed suitable and the women were 'experienced in farm work and supplied at local rate of wages' (p. 65).

Lady Derby, the probable spouse of Lord Derby, who was an important influence in Preston's recruitment, was ensuring that women were able to assist in the effort, particularly in agriculture. As part of her role as chairman of the Lancashire Agriculture Committee, she may have had some involvement with their work. The committee, in conjunction with the Board of Trade Labour Exchanges, promoted the employment of women in agriculture and horticultural work. A letter was forwarded to the Parks and Baths Committee to

> entertain the proposal of training a limited number of women so that they may be of some use in this national emergency … It would not, of course, be possible to give them a long training as they are wanted at once, but they will be of indefinitely more use to those willing to employ them if they had only a short experience in a garden, than if they are absolutely untrained. The Lancashire County Council are already giving free courses in Agriculture, etc., at their Farm near Preston, the pupils finding their own board and lodgings.
>
> (CBP 31/8, p. 334)

The letter was addressed to the Parks and Baths Committee in August 1915, and they later resolved 'that arrangements be left in the hands of the Park Superintendent' (p. 336). Despite such efforts, the agricultural industry was not being helped by the confusion and lack of protection from the War Office, especially in the tribunals, although men who were called up for service and subsequently considered unfit were often assigned work in the fields for the duration of the war.⁹ In March 1915, one Sergeant Rawcliffe stated that he preferred working back on the farms to being billeted with his company.

However, some workforces were exempt under the 'starring' scheme. Arthur Procter Cartmell wrote that on 6 May 1916 a government inspector 'checked our badged men' and reported that 'everything [was] satisfactory to him'. It perhaps helped that the company was providing work for the Ministry of Munitions.

* * *

The tribunals were set up under the Derby Scheme to provide a method of appeal for those men called up to serve; this was continued right through the war. Three tribunals were set up in Preston, but only one dealt with its rural areas. It was evident here that as the war years continued, the tribunal members would get tougher on those cases that were put before them. Appeals were heard from conscientious objectors, one such case being an Ashton market gardener, and his brother, who would rather be 'hung, drawn, and quartered' than take a life in any form. The ensuing conversation suggests that this type of application may not have been tolerated:

> Mr Hubberstey: You breed pigs for killing, don't you?
> Applicant: I don't kill myself. Besides, there is a difference between killing pigs and men.
> Mr Hubberstey: Are you English?
> Applicant: Preston born.
> Mr Hubberstey: Then you're soft.

To further illustrate the tribunal member's point, the applicant's claim was rejected and his brother was given conditional exemption (see the *Preston Guardian*, 13 March 1916). These types of cases would eventually be dealt with by a tribunal that specialised in the cases of conscientious objectors. Those cases that were being heard in early 1916 were those for single men; as part of the Derby Scheme, married men were to be called up last in the groups.

Those cases that were heard in the rural tribunals were often those self-employed or from employers who needed their labour. Applications were also applied for by mothers, but unless the tribunal could be persuaded there was little chance of success.

> They [serving soldiers] only got a shilling a day. She [step-mother] could only draw for one boy, a few shillings a week. She even had to go to court [a military tribunal] when her youngest one went. She had apprenticed him to a printer and bookbinders in Corporation Street. The next one, my own brother, was apprenticed to painting and decorating; they had all been given a trade. She said at court that she had been bringing them up to a trade, although they didn't have a big wage. He said at court, 'I don't care!' Did she call him some names! He said, 'I don't care if you had twenty apprentices! You don't get a penny!' She was upset when she came home! Us girls were keeping the home.

The Women's Land Army
Parade on Fishergate Hill.
(Lancashire Lantern: 4975)

Members of the Women's
Land Army among the
crowd outside Preston's
Public Hall. (Lancashire
Lantern: 4976)

This dramatised photo of
a Land Army member on a
tractor could be illustrating
the point that women were
capable of agriculture work.
(Lancashire Lantern: 4978)

Unfortunately, the mother was only awarded one son's allowance; it was very difficult financially; '[as] the war dragged on and on, it was terrible'.[10] A second contemporary also commented that his mother 'drew five shillings a week which would be a lot'.[11] A further contemporary remembers 'serving all these queues of soldiers ... [who were probably sending or getting pay. In addition,] we paid out allowances for the war. All the war wives and all the Navy women came [to the post office].'[12]

The standard weekly allowance paid to single men who had dependants was 5s. It was set by the government Pay and Allowance Regulations. In fact it was estimated by the council that £115 alone would be spent on the allowances for the financial year from 31 March 1915 to 31 March 1916 (CBP 20/38, p. 45).

One contemporary may believe that this amount was fair, but for others it would depend on the size of the family, whether there were other family members working to provide more income, and expenditures such as rent. We cannot forget that food prices were continually increasing, particularly the price of milk, which kept rising every few months (DDX 1706/1/4).

Some may have even been jealous of other people's incomes, although there does seem to be a rather large consensus that things were difficult financially in the home: 'Other people were now earning big money on munition work and food, unrationed, became very dear.'[13] It could be suggested that this sort of thinking was what made companies such as Horrockses, Dick, Kerr & Co. and even Preston Borough Council, at the onset of war, want to support their workers financially, or at least in the eyes of the public (see the beginning of chapter 2).

A contemporary who served in the First World War recalled, 'I joined the Artillery and we had 1s 2.5d a day and out of that you made an allotment [allowance] of 6d and I think my mother got 12s 11d, I think, that's what she got while I were away ... No [it wasn't much].' A soldiers' income, however, was not always reliable, or useful to him: 'I used to get 5s 0d one week and 4s 0d the next four. Then when we got in France we had another 6d a day proficiency as a signaller and then I got a stripe. But as soon as we went across we went to Ypres. Well, we never got paid for about three months. It was no use to you, you couldn't spend it. There was nothing there.'[14]

* * *

The concern for the time went beyond protecting the agricultural labourers. 'In the schemes for enlistment ... special regard should be paid to the needs of the cotton trade,' said the Preston mayor at the annual Preston Traders' Mutual Dinner, which had been covered by the *Preston Guardian* on 25 November 1915, 'and that all those who were essential to carrying on of that trade should be exempt. He [Cartmell] hoped that if a man was found to be necessary as an engineer in a cotton works, he hoped he would remain there, and not be found working at Dick, Kerr's later on [making munitions]; and also as they were taking such extraordinary pains to keep women employed in the mills, and not try their apprentice hands in the Pay Office of elsewhere.' Dick, Kerr & Co. was the first company in Preston to convert their factory to helping the war effort. According to Harry Cartmell, they converted their factory to shell production and in doing so relinquished their own business in late October 1914. He comments that they made 3.25 million projectiles over the course of the four years of the war (p. 117), J. H. Price's *The Dick, Kerr Story* (1993) provides further figures for Dick, Kerr's defence work, perhaps for one year's orders: '100 petrol-electric locomotives; 500 cable drums; 151 pontoon bridges; 500 chassis for wagons; 95 pontoons; 60 bodies for Maudsley lorries; 300 general service wagons; 2,500 cartridge boxes; 72 timber wagons; 30,000 pairs of horseshoes; 75 pontoon boats' (p. 46).

* * *

As part of the Derby Scheme, protection for the workforces of key industries was provided; those trades that were vital to the war effort were 'starred' and those that weren't were 'unstarred'. The original system took shape when the men were doing the original canvassing for Derby's grouping scheme in November 1915. On 6 November 1915, the *Preston Guardian* reported that as many as 12,000 cards were distributed among those who were to undertake the canvass. They were under the supervision of the town clerk and the two men acting as secretaries to Preston's Recruitment Committee, which had been set up early in the war with its headquarters at the Harris Free Library.

In the creation of the canvassing scheme, a method of appeal was created for men to apply for exemption from attestation or, failing that, for the postponement of their calling up on grounds of personal hardship or essential war work. Locally, tribunals were created to hear these cases and there was some opposition to the impartiality of their members.

The *Preston Guardian* reported on 20 November 1916 that a number of Lancashire MPs representing industrial constituencies conferred with Lord Derby in a meeting at the War Office. The meeting was held because businessmen were opposed to the large number of lawyers on a tribunal that was to consider what men were irreplaceable in manufacture. At the conclusion of the meeting, Lord Derby promised that the composition of the tribunals would be considered and agreed that labour interests should be represented on the tribunal as well.

Applications were not just being held by tribunals for recruitment proposes, but for working in munitions also.

Those committees were just as harsh, and whether you got exemption could come down to your skills and the trade you did before the war, and sometimes luck. Apparently, the family story was that my father [a pattern maker in Barrow] was the only one considered versatile enough to do this. The other pattern makers were all called up and never came back. My dad never went to war [he had the talent to turn to hand drawings for hand grenades and bombs]. He was in a protected job because he was working on munitions. I think there was a story [that] went … that the factory had to change over from its normal products to munitions and he was the only one that was sufficiently well trained to be able to do it.

Health and age were other factors that were perhaps taken into consideration: 'My dad continued more or less to run the place on his £3 a week. The excuse for this, to an extent, was that his health had begun to crack up.'[15] The situation at home may also have been a factor, particularly if someone worked in a protected industry. 'He [Helen's father] was exempt. With me being a weaver I was exempt and my mother was a winder and she was exempt. We did our best at whatever was coming.'[16]

Some male workers went into munitions for the higher wages as their current job was not paying enough; munitions offered a wage of around £2 or £3.[17] 'When he [my father] came to Preston the 1914 War had started then and he went basket making for ammunitions baskets ... he was there for a long time ... I know it [the wage] wasn't anything fantastic. I mean we didn't retire with fortunes because all these munition people, they were private concerns, they were family concerns, they didn't belong to big companies, not in those days.' However, 'some of the firms, it [the war] made them. I mean, the one my dad worked for that was a private concern, a foundry, old established firm and they certainly made their money during the war but I don't think they passed it on to the work people. I don't think for a moment they did but it certainly made them.'[18]

There is evidence of a Preston firm being in discussion with the War Office about being taken over. In the business diary for his timber and building company, Arthur Procter Cartmell recorded on 4 September 1916, 'Application [received] from Ministry of Munitions for particulars re controlling our works.' He adds that a reply was sent 6 September, but no mention of a decision was made. On 9 October 1916 it was stated, 'No reply from M of M re painting tin linings.' A reply was received and negotiations over price took place, the writer, probably with a lack of patience, writing, 'Failing a reply by the 9th ... we should commence delivery unpainted.' No reply was received in the three-day period for the 2d offer. Further War Office contracts were for rifle ranges in Liverpool in March 1916, which involved the production of 4,000 4.5-inch ammunition boxes, at a price of 4s 10d each. An enquiry was also received from the War Office for a new aeroplane shed, '140-0 x 65-0', at Southport; a tender was sent for £2,310 on 19 July 1916. Further negotiations took place on orders for ammunition boxes in 1917 and 1918. Contracts were also received from individuals; for example, on 22 September 1916 the company received a telephone order from Captain Harrison, requesting concrete foundations for two anti-aircraft guns at Barrow.

* * *

A second contemporary, aged around eleven in 1914, concurs with the above experiences of working in a munitions factory, but he does so by comparing it with his experiences of employment in a mill. 'I only made two or three pounds, that was all ... It [working in munitions] was better than working in the mill. You were more active than being in the mill. Because looking back at different jobs in the mill, the heat and the smell and being sat down at the stool, it just wasn't the job.'[19] The company was also an employer of women, much like Horrockses, as seen above. For those that worked there it was 'only a wartime job. I think it was 1919 when they got finished up.'

A pair of women work
on a section of machinery
in a Horrockses factory.
(Lancashire Lantern: 4974)

A view of a Horrockses
factory floor that clearly
shows the scale of the
munitions work and the
number of staff required, both
male and female. (Lancashire
Lantern: 4951)

A stockpile of munitions.
(Lancashire Lantern: 4952)

The tasks that were demanded of the women workers were not easy, even if the worker was a 'sturdy well-built person', especially if it was 'packing projectiles in cases'.[20]

Some women could not be removed from their position at home and the money that was being sent to support them. One woman still could not afford to raise five children, even with an army allowance of 27-/d, so she had to balance working the night shift with bringing up the children.[21] However, having a father away at the munitions and the mother left at home to raise the children was at least an enjoyable experience for one child; the father 'was miserable … bad-tempered and wasn't worth living with … He went away to work at Vickers Armstrong's at Barrow in the 1914–1918 War and it was the time of our lives because he was away … he used to come home every second or third weekend … he could have got a job here [in Preston].' As seen with other families, having a parent away at the munitions meant the family, particularly the wife, struggled: 'My mother was left with the kids and the shop and the rations and the lot. I remember during that time I hardly ever went to school.'[22] But it wasn't always the mother who was left to struggle, as the eldest female sibling might have to take over: 'I recall my sister Louise a lot about this time; she being the eldest was very aware of mum's hard times and she "stood in" as best she could for both parents. I remember her making us go to bed at nights, many times after a chase.'[23] For some, family could not be relied upon. 'My mother used to say that with three children and the pittance that she got from my father's allowance, she didn't know how she would have got through the war as her family had given her no assistance at all … I remember my mother often saying that if it hadn't been for Eadie Duckworth coming round and giving her a hand and perhaps letting her get out shopping, she didn't know how she would have managed. When she went out shopping, I was the eldest, and she would take me with her and probably Eadie Duckworth would look after the two young ones … I would only be about six then.'[24]

However, not all families struggled to make ends meet, even if the husband or father was away at war: 'Because my grandmother was living with her … Yes [my mother] was working. And then our Maggie were working, my eldest sister were working and I didn't think they did so bad … We always did [give mum our wages] … Oh yes. That was the thing. You couldn't do [it] any other way. There was no such thing as boarding. You gave the lot.'[25] There was also

the simple reason that mother had a better wage weaving … [her wages went up] automatically, yes. Where, normally, people had two looms, well there was always four of them … [because there was a shortage of workers] More so in the '14–'18 War than the last one [the Second World War] because they never moved them about the same. No, they [women from Preston] wouldn't [leave to go and work on munitions elsewhere] because we had the munitions depots here in what is now English Electric [formerly Dick, Kerr & Co. till 1919] and that kind of thing. They took them locally. And if there was any movement then we [children] weren't old enough to take at notice of it.[26]

Another contemporary recalled,

> The First World War broke out and we lived in Holstein Street and my sister lived in East
> Street. They had a bath and we hadn't. Her husband had gone to India so the landlord
> said, it was five shillings a week in that house, and the landlord said he would soon get
> another house after the war. We said, 'Come on mother, let's go, they have a bath.' So we
> went to live with our Annie and as a result we stopped there and we never got another
> house. I got married from there. We used to have some fun.[27]

* * *

On Moor Park, opposite the football stadium, it was decided to build a Voluntary Aid
Detachment (VAD) hospital just after the start of the war. It was opened in January 1915
and the early structures were provided by the Royal Lancashire Agriculture Society in
the form of a pavilion that held thirty-five patients. Additional structures were added
over the course of the war to create new wards, and new equipment was also installed
in them. (For further information on the evolution of the hospital see Martin Kevill
(ed.), *The Personal Diary of Nurse de Trafford: 1916–1920*, The Book Guild Ltd, pp.
146–147.) Such improvements were usually a result of charity; for example, the staff at
Horrockses raised funds for the hospital; the Horrockses chairman Lord Hollins and
his wife were also patrons of the hospital. A further addition was added when Grove
House, on the junction of Moor Park Avenue and Garstang Road, became an annex of
the hospital in early 1918, holding twenty-eight patients. One observer recalled that 'the
wounded soldiers all wore light-blue uniforms. You could see them walking about with
broken arms and legs'.[28] The injuries to individuals would have been a striking reminder
that the war was destructive and vicious, something that the next chapter will show.

The Moor Park Hospital. (Lancashire Lantern: 1525)

Wounded men posing cheerfully for a photo despite their injuries. (Preston Digital Archive)

Another view of the extended Moor Park Hospital. (Preston Digital Archive)

4

NEWS FROM THE FRONT LINE

We are to have a 'Bloody battle' on the morrow.[1]

'Personally, I find it almost impossible [to eat], for the thought of fighting my first battle on the morrow has made me far too excited, so that I do not get more than an hour['s sleep]. I think that my only wish was that I should … turn about and run – I felt like it just then.' These were the thoughts of an unnamed lieutenant in the war diary of the 1st Battalion Loyal North Lancashire Regiment, part of the 1st Division, I Corps, British Expeditionary Force (BEF). The battalion's first involvement began

at daybreak [on 24 August 1914, when] we got ready for the attack [at the Battle of Mons]. The guns commenced at the first streak of dawn, and I … particularly noticed one of our batteries on ahead of us. The Germans had found the range and were planting their shells just over the battery; it was being corrected each time and they were gradually getting right on the guns. It was the first and last time I saw our guns in the open without any cover … We were told to retire about half a mile, and thus we began the famous retreat.

* * *

Monday 1914

My Dear Mother,

We are leaving at about 7 o'clock this evening, being the last in the [51st Highland] Division to do so.

We have no idea where we are sailing from. We may be two or three days en route so don't be anxious if you don't hear from me for a few days. I will send you a [postcard] as soon as we get across at the earliest opportunity.

Just going to have high tea before we leave.

At present am looking like 'the Dartmoor Shepheard' having had a close crop.

Dearest love to all,

Your affectionate son,

Leslie

In writing another letter home, Captain Duckworth, of Ribby Hall, Kirkham, who had been one of the few officers at the front for fourteen months without a break, described the details of an attack that the 1st/2nd Battalion Loyal North Lancashire was involved in:

Friday June 17th 1915

My dearest Mother and Father,

Hope you received my note dispatched last night. I sent it express so that you would receive it before the casualty lists appeared.

We made an attack on Wednesday night and how I have escaped I don't know. It was absolute hell I can tell you. Shells were bursting every yard and clouds of bullets were flying about. I hope I never see such another sight in my life. Am glad to say there are a few of us unscathed, Capt[ain] Booth, Major Foley, Lindsay, Rennard, Capt[ain] Widdows and [Rudolf] Ord are the only ones that have come through untouched so you can tell we got pretty well knocked about. We shall probably be out for some time now as we shall want reorganising and a lot of area to fill up.

I had some wonderful escapes, having two bullets through my cap. At present I am acting Adjutant as Capt[ain] Norman is badly wounded; our [Commanding Officer] got a bullet through the nose and is temp[orarily] out of action. It was a pitiful sight yesterday morning when we brought out the remainder [of the battalion because] everybody's clothes were torn with the barbed wire and we did look a mess I can tell you.

I received your parcel last night there are so few of us now that we have a combined mess. So don't send any more tinned goods as there are plenty in stock. A few cakes … and [some] chocolate … will be very welcome.

I must close now

With dearest love to all

Your affectionate son, Leslie

The following is from the battalion war diary and is quoted in the 1921 *War History of the 1st/2nd Battalion*, this being part of the Loyal North Lancashire Regiment:

At 6 p.m. [On Tuesday 15 August 1914] C Company charged from the fire trench … They had to climb the parapet, and, under a withering fire, form to the left flank slightly, and then charge. They did this almost perfectly in line, and were in possession if the trench inside three minutes. Their losses were chiefly from rifle and machine gun fire. This must have been principally from the main trench, and not the advanced trench of the salient, since they found most of the Germans there sheltering in their dugouts; these were dealt with by bombing parties … When the trench was won, comparatively easily, the Germans holding up their hands and pleading for mercy, the bombing parties extended outwards [into other trenches and] … actually beyond the road so fast that their bayonet men could not keep up with them. They mostly ran along the top of the trench, with the German and British artillery both bombarding the lines all this time very heavily indeed.

Red screens were used to show the furthermost point reached by the infantry, to enable the artillery to support … [But] About 11 p.m. there was a slackening of the German fire, both artillery and rifle. There was uncertainty as to the actual position

A postcard from a soldier at the front to someone in Preston. Note the 'on active service' message. (Preston Digital Archive)

of the attacking battalions ... and [at the same time as] asking for instructions ... the German counter-attack began and prevented the instructions arriving. It ... began by bombing ... so severely that the machine gun there was damaged and put out of action ... Almost at the same time, the Germans began to bomb down the right communication trench ... and followed this by throwing bombs across the open. There was no means of replying, and no cover to be had anywhere in the ditch. To stay there would have meant wiping out of those on the line ... Orders were given, therefore, to retire from the position ... The casualties were heavy ... [420 NCOs killed, missing or wounded, and a complete battalion strength of 520 out of a possible 1,000]. The British report of June 16th issued by the Press Bureau [sums up the above action]: 'Yesterday evening, we captured the German front line trenches east of Festubert, a mile of front, but failed to hold them during the night against the strong counter-attacks delivered by the enemy.'

(pp. 14–20)

* * *

'Operation orders received on possible advance [24 September 1915].' This was the first action that the 7th Battalion of the Loyal North Lancashire would be involved in; it was at the Battle of Loos. The war diary continued, 'A few enemy shells fell near Bn H.Q. during the night 23/24th but none of them burst. Our bombardment continued all day.' However, the following morning, near Rue De L'Epinette, the battalion stood to arms at 4-30 a.m: messages re impending gas and smoke attack received at 5.7 a.m. At 5-50 a.m. an intense bombardment began ... [Until 6 a.m.] the whole front of the Brigade was covered with white smoke. The bombardment continued violently until 6-30 a.m. ... [However, the battalion was in reserve at this point and did not move into the front line until 28 September 1915.] The enemy were very quiet all night: except that at 4 a.m. they threw about twenty bombs into the Orchard Sailent ... Considerable work was [soon] done at clearing up and draining trenches.

(pp. 13–14)

The battalion were not involved in any advance, their role being to defend the line, but the Germans were still active over the coming days as there were regular reports of mining and patrols being sent out, as well as random artillery barrages and the throwing of bombs.

Writing from the front line, Sergeant Rawcliffe commented on 26 September 1915,

Dear Old Molly,

Still alive and kicking and guzzling when I get the chance and starving when I've got to go short [rations]. I think we are doing fairly well out here and have had marvellous luck so far as some have got it hot compared with us. I am dead scared of being mistaken for a Russian as we haven't got our razors this trip and I have got whiskers that would put a barbed wire entanglement to shame. You would laugh if you could see us in our little dugout living happily underground. The blooming artillery banging away at night shakes the dickens out of you, especially when the very big ones go off.

Your little brother Billy

His next letter was written on 2 October:

Somewhere in France

My dear sister,

I got your welcome parcel just as we were marching for the trenches, and as one chap put it, we have been through hell with the lid off and yet these old stagers tell us we haven't smelt it properly. It is God help us when we have to rough it, if we haven't started yet. I will write and tell you our experiences when we get safely out. We are sincerely hoping we get sent back to rest before long as we are jolly well played out. I have got a few minutes and am dashing this off in a dugout and am expecting to be called out any minute. I am too soft-hearted to be a sergeant as I fairly don't like to keep turning lads out when they are dead beat as they have been working night and day lately, and yet we have to do it.

This is a nice dugout and there is only me and the lad who looks after me and boils my tea. I got a photo of Dick [his brother] this morning and he does look champion, how I wish I was with him ... We have been up to our knees in mud for the last four or five days with sandbags on either leg. My whiskers would have passed me for a Russian. Our clothes were all mud. I would have given anything for you to have seen me as I was before I managed to borrow a razor for a shave, so I really look nutty tonight.

Soldiers of the Loyal North Lancashire in the trenches. (Lancashire Lantern: 4978)

I do bless you when your parcels and letters keep rolling up. You are a little champion and if you think half as much of me as I do of you I shall be satisfied ... Well I'm all aches and pains with writing all this. Love to all the family.

Your loving brother, Billy

His next letter dated 12 October had a darker tone. It contained some news:

Dear old Molly,

You know the Rev. Lancaster of Inskip church, his son [Corporal] Geoff [Connell], is in our company, he was killed last night as well as one or two others. I think he was the only son and such a grand lad and a full corporal. We were big pals with living so near together. We often used to speak about home places ... We get rum rations now and the other day I had to stand guard with a corporal to see no-one came twice, so near the finish I said to the corporal my feet are cold and of course he said so are mine. At the finish the Captain said better have another dose, Rawcliffe, to warm your feet, so we two got double, and by gum I could hardly get along the trench. I went diving into my dug out and didn't I feel rotten next day. I haven't touched it since.

Billy

* * *

It was in the following year, at the Battle of the Somme, that the 7th Battalion would be involved in action outside of the trench. The actions of one particular company are of importance: D Company was the Preston Pals. Sergeant Rawcliffe was in fact an original member of the Pals; he had returned from New Zealand before the war and enlisted with his two brothers, who were serving in different regiments to him. Rawcliffe wrote again from the trenches, on 10 July 1916, of the harsh reality of war, as well as the activities of the Pals, in the early days of the Battle of the Somme:

> Dear Mother and James,
>
>   Well you need not be anxious about me as we have been in the mix-up and came through safely, although I can tell you I said my prayers often enough. A number of fine chaps went up with us and didn't come back. I was lucky as chaps were hit alongside me but I wasn't touched. They seem to think our mob did good work whilst we were there. We got quite a few prisoners and it was laughable to see one big German, he must have been nearly seven foot tall coming down between two of our little chaps, it looked funny I tell you ... I lost the officer that I thought so much of, he was trying to get a wounded man in when he was shot. I nearly blubbered as I thought the world of him. Thank goodness I was there and helped to get him in but he never spoke after he was hit as he was dead in about a minute. Poor chap, he had a heart of gold and was brave as a lion and had just been recommended for bravery. I might say without boasting I would have taken a big risk for him. I shall always be thankful I was there to help bandage him and carry him in. McIllwaine was there as he was his orderly and poor old Mac was upset. Mac and I and the Sgt Major got him in ... I know you won't mind me telling you I haven't had a bean in my pocket for the last eight days. We couldn't have spent it anyway. The first time I have been broke in France but we are getting paid today ...
>
>   Yours to a cinder,
>   Billy

His next letter, on 14 July, was unfortunately his last, and he commented, 'We are in perfect safety at present and we are getting very good reports here so cheers, perhaps the war will soon be over.' He even commented about his commission finally coming through and going to cadet school in October – 'if all goes well and I live long enough of course'. This optimism was short-lived, as the following was written at 2.35 a.m. on the morning of 23 July 1916 in the 7th Battalion war diary:

> D Coy also had heavy casualties. Report received from 2 Lt Tovani that Capt Thompson and 2 Lt Hoyle were killed. The Coy had got to within a few yards of the German front line trench, but was again held up by M[achine] guns. Being unable to get on 2 Lieut Tovani withdrew the remainder of the Coy (about fifty men) to our front line.

In a letter to Sergeant Rawcliffe's parents on 25 July 1916, an anonymous participant at the advance at Bazentine-le-Petit wrote,

We were told that we had to take the German front line and about one o'clock on Sunday night we mounted the attack. All went well till we were just about 20 yards from the German front line, then our chaps began to fall round me. It was awful. I was next to Sgt Rawcliffe. All at once he fell hit in the side. At that time everybody got down so I was able to attend to him. I got him in a shell hole with the help of another sergeant. We bandaged him up, then we had to withdraw. It was awful to leave him for we had always been pals but it could not be helped. I went back to our line to find him; we had been cut up badly. Later on in the afternoon Sgt Rawcliffe crawled in. It took him five hours. I helped to carry him to the dressing station. The doctor said he was alright as far as we know. [However, he later died from the gunshot wound to his stomach.]

Private Mawbey, another survivor of the conflict, wrote in his memoirs, 'It was bad enough getting through our own wire in the dark. I spent the next day with two other blokes cowering in a shellhole and got back with a whole skin' (p. 18). These accounts certainly do suggest that the Preston Pals were involved in a conflict that may have caused large amount of casualties. Even Mayor Cartmell commented about the huge loss in his speech at the Tradesman Dinner in November 1916: 'How could we bear the knowledge of what has happened to the Preston Pals, that splendid company of fine young fellows, full of fire and life and energy, that left the town in the very early days of the War?' (p. 243) However, despite the evidence above and even that of local opinion, the Preston Pals were not slaughtered at Bazentine-le-Petit. I have argued this in the updated dissertation I wrote on the Preston Pals when I was at University – it is available digitally on my website.

* * *

On the morning of 3 April 1916, the 13th Division, of which the 6th Battalion Loyal North Lancashire was a part, was to assault the trenches at El Hanna, but owing to the sodden state of the roads the attack had to be postponed until 5 April. Major W. G. Cragg DSO shares his experiences of the Mesopotamia assault:

All movement took place at night and all tents were left standing at Sheikh Saad, but the Turk knew full well that we were preparing to assault Hannah. He had Command of the Air and could not have failed to notice troops massed in the several lines of our position there ... Our attack was timed to take place at 4-55 a.m., 5 minutes before dawn, at which time also our Artillery opened on their support trenches and vantage points. Our first line was detailed to take the enemy front line trench, and 2nd line [to take the] enemy's second line and our 3rd and 4th lines to capture his 3rd line which was about 800 yards behind his 1st line, i.e. we played leap frog. The L. N. Lancs were in the last line and it looked as if we should have the toughest job. The troops were extraordinarily eager for the fight and it was a hard job to keep them back and wait till our guns had lifted once the assault was launched. The Turks had withdrawn the bulk of his force and only held the front line, which was not strongly held. They had very few machine guns in it and not many infantry. The trenches here were roughly 100 yards apart, and we had comparatively few casualties considering the number of troops assaulting ... We killed a certain number of Turks and took a few prisoners, but the majority bolted when they saw us coming and could afterwards have been seen wading through open water on their way back to their next position at Falahiyeh. Our progress across the Hannah position was necessarily slow, as every trench taken was at once consolidated, since we, during the early stage at least, had no means of knowing whether the Turks were holding it in force in one of their lines further back. However, we quickly concluded the enemy had evacuated the whole position as we could see our red (artillery) flag bearers pressing on and after a time our only casualties were from our own guns, which were not lifting quickly enough and into whose bursts our too impetuous infantry were now running. Our red flags were carried by the most advanced infantry and were to be stuck in the ground to denote the furthermost point our attacking troops had reached. The signal for artillery to lift was to denoted by the waving backwards and forwards of the flag. Later on, owing to our flags being captured and the Turks using them for their own ends, the colour, shape or design has had to be changed for every fresh assault. Thus ended the battle of El Hannah.

(pp. 32–33)

* * *

'Farewell to Mespot' by Arthur Smith, 6th Battalion Loyal North Lancashire:

Our kits are packed and ready,
And we're as happy as can be,
For its back to dear old Blighty,
And the folks we long to see.
The sun can scorch and blister,
And the dust may swirl and choke,
But we'd rather be in Blighty,
'Mid the noisy looms and smoke.
The palms, friends, wave a greeting,
And beckon us to stay,
But the memories of the homeland,
Are calling us away.
We can see the Tigris moving
With ceaseless silent flood
But the Boulds-worth hills smell sweeter
And the good old wycollar mud.
We've fed on ration biscuits,
And we've drunk the Tigris neat,
We've slithered through the mud and rain
And frizzled in the heat.
We've felt the sandflies biting,
At mosquitoes oft we've swore,
Goodbye, you little devils,
You'll trouble us no more.
We've seen Baghdad and Basra.
Viewed minaret and dome

But we'd swop the blooming country
For afoot of land at home.
We've camped in desert places,
Where howling jackals run,
We've cursed the Wily Arab,
And the Jurk and ruddy Hun.
We've passed through Kut and Kurnah.
Where Adam and Eve fell
But there ain't no Figs or Apples
And it's as hot as Hell.
In olden days when vexed or wrath
We spoke of regions hot,
And we muttered Hades!, now we'll say,
Oh! Go to Mesopot.
We've given the joyful optic,
To the Dancing girls – hot stuff,
But what price the Hardcastle Crags
With a dainty bit of fluff.
Were fed up with all their cafes
And bazaars where Arabs scrawl
We're longing for old Market Street

And to see Wigan Town Hall.
Oh! Eden you're the limit,
Farewell thou barren spot,
And heaven grant we never more
Set foot in Mesopot.

Using the Harris Roll of Honour forms we can show that certain years of the war might have hit Preston harder than others. The forms contained information such as name, address, occupation, place of death, date of death and a comments section. These forms were produced in order for relatives, employers or even spouses to get the name of an individual who had died onto the town's roll of honour. Many, however, were not fully completed and names were sometimes submitted twice for consideration. In his *A Worthy Monument: The Story of Preston's War Memorial 1917 to 1927*, compiled 2006, John Garlington explains that 'there certainly had been no rush and forms had been available for relatives for ten years. There had been frequent reminders and announcements, with the lists of names always open for inspection' (p. 18). See the final chapter for further details on remembrance.

Years and numbers of the deaths of Preston servicemen

Year	1914	1915	1916	1917	1918	1919	1920	1921	1922	1923	1924
Number	105	242	440	494	472	34	12	7	3	1	3

Source: The Preston Roll of Honour Forms

Preston serviceman deaths by month in 1916

Month	Total	Month	Total
January	7	July	93
February	8	August	88
March	9	September	64
April	45	October	39
May	25	November	31
June	21	December	10

Source: The Preston Roll of Honour Forms.

A completed roll of honour form. (LCC Cultural Services and Preston City Council)

5

WHILE YOU'RE AWAY

But if only you may be allowed to come back eventually I will gladly wait even years. I always feel so perfectly happy when you are here, I never wish for anything else.[1]

In 1918, close to the end of the war, rationing of certain foods was introduced following the successes of some German submarines in sinking ships carrying imports into Britain. A contemporary recalled that things were not just difficult at the end of the war, as his mother

> used to go out shopping … during the war, she just couldn't get hold of anything, particularly after standing in a queue. I remember [as a child] these women with all these wicker baskets and they would stand in this queue and there would always be a policeman controlling the queue and then suddenly the cut-off point came and the policeman used to wade in roughly and disperse the women, not with truncheons but roughly. I have seen my mother crying many a time when she hasn't been able to get anything. In other words, she has gone out with an empty basket and has come back home with a empty basket. She had three children to keep, this would be after her father who was living with her had died of a stroke … It wasn't a question of finance in the war, it was a question of availability of supplies, as in the Second World War, the stuff wasn't always there. My aunt, if she was not on duty at [Fulwood] hospital, would sometimes get the three children their breakfast and she used to make one egg do for three by making it into sandwiches. If by any chance mother managed to get another egg or two, it would be two between three but I never remember having a whole egg except at Easter when you got a whole shell egg to yourself.[2]

In those days our mothers didn't have shopping bags, everything went in their aprons. They picked up their aprons like that. I remember my mother buying flour because she always baked her own bread.[3]

* * *

Mayor Cartmell writes,

> Of all the movements prompted by the war conditions none evoked more enthusiastic service amongst the workers or more willing support from the public than the Sailors' and Soldiers' Refreshment Buffet, established at the Preston Railway Station. One of the busiest wayside stations in England, on the main line midway between London and Scotland, the junction for many important Lancashire towns, Preston afforded special opportunities for offering a welcome to soldiers on their way to or from camp or from overseas. The railway authorities entered whole-heartedly into the scheme, and placed at the disposal of the ladies a commodious room communicating with the two main platforms. From the moment of its dedication to its new purpose on the 19 August, 1915, that room was in continuous use night and day for the benefit of the travelling sailor and soldier. The leading ladies each with a bevy of helpers relieved one another in succession every 12 hours.

> (p. 182)

Its members also had to pay a monthly subscription of 2/6 from 1916, as well as other adhering to other rules of the Sailors' and Soldiers' Buffet (DDX 2182/1; DDX 2061/1). The members included the mayoress (later Dame) Anna Marie Cartmell as president; the Buffet, however, was just one of many projects in which she was involved. It could be suggested that her work may have stemmed from a meeting of ladies that was held in connection with the National Relief Fund, at the Town Hall on 12 August 1914. In attendance was the mayoress, Mrs Wolley, Mrs Jamieson, Mrs Hayhurst, Mrs Meghay, Mrs T. H. Myres, Mrs A. Ranson, Mrs A. Howard, Miss Clemesha, Mrs Howarth, Mrs Carter, Miss Wittam and Mrs Smith. Several issues were resolved, firstly the acceptance of 'a kind offer' from the YMCA of a workroom and secondly that a subcommittee be formed to make arrangements for the making of garments. Unfortunately there are no further entries of this committee, but Mayoress Cartmell was also involved in the resettling of the Belgian refugees (CBP 53/11).

Others members of the Buffet committee included Mrs Todd as chairman of the executive committee, Mrs Foster as vice-chairman, Mrs Eastwood as honorary chairman, Mrs Woodcock as honorary secretary and Mrs Bell, Mrs Blackhurst and Mrs Marcus Rea as other members of the executive committee, with Mrs Threlfall as manageress (DDX 2182/1). Others included Ada Whiteside, along with her sisters May and Floria and her mother Sophie, who acted as volunteers. Their involvement in helping soldiers, however, began early in the war as they had noticed that soldiers with serious injuries were passing through Preston's railway station without any support or aid, particularly that of walking sticks. In response they launched an appeal for walking sticks, which was extraordinarily successful. Many thank-you letters were sent to the family. One happy recipient wrote,

> Raddon Court Red Cross Hospital
> 3rd November 1914

> To the Missess Whiteside,
> Walking sticks arrived safely today for which we thank you very much. We have 33

patients. 19 Belgian soldiers and 14 English. They are all doing well. We shall find the sticks very useful for them, while here, and if we find the men need one we give one to take away, so we shall be glad to apply to you for more if necessary. Thanking you very much for your kind thought and interest in our hospital. I am

    Yours faithfully

    Matron

An inventory list of the numbers of sticks and the places of their delivery is also contained within the collection. In addition, it was reported by the *Preston Guardian* in January 1916 that 250 'helpers are engaged, some of whom come from neighbouring towns, such as Blackburn, Lancaster, Chorley, St Anne's, and Lytham'.

    Cartmell continues,

> In the month of June, 1917, the Committee with characteristic enterprise published a little explanatory pamphlet, from which I venture to take a few extracts.
>
>   The surprising scope of this enterprise can be best seen at night. 'A trainful of "Jocks" arrives in the 'wee sma' hours' and is met by a devoted band of ladies carrying steaming buckets of food, which rapidly disappear under the attacks made upon them. Again, if you look into the Buffet itself, you will find a number of weary mud-stained men stretched out fast asleep, only on forms, but provided with a rug and pillow and duly labelled with the time at which their train goes. Others may be seen either reading the magazines and papers which are provided, or making use of the notepaper supplied to them – a privilege most highly valued – to write those wonderful cheery letters in which everyone seems to have but one object – to make light of his own discomfort and to comfort the hearts of the people at home.' One can imagine the sensation of a battalion of soldiers with many hours of travelling behind them, and, as many before them, suddenly finding themselves objects of solicitude and attention on the part of a small army of young women pressing upon them warm food.
>
> (pp. 182–183)

Mayor Cartmell comments that the women workers were often drafted into other occupations, so most of the work of the Buffet was done by the housewives of the town. He adds that in the week before Christmas 1916, 12,449 men were served in thirty-six hours. Furthermore, the average of men served in January 1917 was 3,250 every twenty-four hours. When the Soldiers' Buffet was closed down on 31 May 1919, it was found that it had served over 3 million men (p. 184). We should look to those that worked, and volunteered their time, to the Soldiers' Buffet for the reason for this success. Cartmell agrees:

> The ladies of the Buffet were fortunate in having their reward in this life. They walked (if their nimble movements may be so described) by sight and not, as so many others, by faith, and the glad thanks of the men to whom they had the opportunity of ministering must have proved ample and prompt repayment for the sacrifices involved.

Fishergate, early twentieth century. (Preston Digital Archive)

Friargate, early twentieth century. (Preston Digital Archive)

Running the Buffet was costly, especially in the purchasing of food as the prices kept increasing as the war progressed – an increase from which the Soldier's Buffet was not exempt. For example, the weekly cost of food in June 1917 was £70, but it later grew to over £100. Cartmell points out, with some humour, 'that the [Soldier's Buffet] committee never found reason to complain that the cruse was running dry'. The reason for this was because of the subscriptions that it was receiving. Cartmell provides figures, although he does not state for what period. The figures he provides are either for 1917 or the whole war:

Summary of Subscriptions, &c.:

	£	s	d
Heads and Helpers	1,061	4	11
Civilians	657	7	11
Donations	11,017	15	5
Gift Depot	503	9	6
Fête Fund	2,908	9	1
Total	16,148	6	10

(p. 184)

The activities of the Soldiers' Buffet were not unique, however; indeed, they may have been inspired by the work of other voluntary organisations. Firstly, a refreshment stall was set up on Watling Street Road, near Fulwood Barracks itself, in August 1914 during the accommodation crisis that had seen soldiers sleeping where they could, even in private households. The scale of this stall's popularity was revealed in a letter submitted to the *Preston Guardian* in September 1914. It stated, 'In the course of one week we supplied over 13,000 buns, and over 16,000 cups of tea and coffee, in addition to large quantities of sandwiches, meat pies, &c.' It adds that this generosity was continued by the Fulwood Soldiers' Welfare Committee at Kitchener's Pavilion. Kitchener's Pavilion was the name of a large timber building located on the edge of Moor Park near Deepdale Road. The *Preston Guardian* reported in October 1914 that the pavilion was designed to be a home of sorts and it was intended to be 'a cosy place' for recruits. It possessed a kitchen that provided refreshments at a reasonable price, and an on-site post office, which meant that soldiers could write and send postcards. The pavilion also provided magazines and other reading materials for the recruits and it must have been genuinely popular, considering it was visited on a daily basis by 3,000–4,000 recruits. The refreshment stall on Watling Street Road seems to have expanded in size, as by late August it was reported by the *Preston Herald* that both women and gentlemen from the garrison and Fulwood parish church were serving food in tents. Other wartime organisations included the Citizen Rifle Corps. Another example was given by the *Preston Guardian* in January 1916:

The local branch of the Prisoners of War Help Society has 'adopted' some 260 Loyal North Lancashire men who are prisoners in Germany, and sends out to them parcels of food, clothing and comforts fortnightly. A committee of Ladies of Preston, Fulwood, Ashton,

Sleeping accommodation in the interior of the Buffet. (Lancashire Record Office: DDX 2061/1)

and Farington, with Mrs Cuthbert Pyke as secretary, pack and send parcels weekly (to half the 'adopted' men adopted weeks) from the Preston Guild Hall. Special parcels were sent to each man for Christmas. Altogether there are 630 men of this regiment who are prisoners of war in the various 'Gefangenenlager' (internment camps) in Germany, the rest of which has been 'adopted' by similar committees of ladies in various parts of the country. The central society supplies information with respect to the camps in Germany, and arranged for the distribution of the parcels sent, helped by the American Ambassadors, and there is ample evidence that the comforts sent from home reach the men in Germany.

* * *

Whilst St. Joseph's Hospital – like all other charitable institutions – has suffered from the financial pressure caused by the war which has raged during the latter half of the year, it has nevertheless progressed, has become more widely known, and by extending its sphere of uselessness has raised itself to a more fitting position amongst the other institutions of the town, those devoted to the treatment and relief of disease, and the assistance of the poor in time of trouble and distress.

For a long time the want of a sufficient supply of beds for male patients has been keenly felt ... The large room situated under the Chapel, and extending its length, offered all the requirements of an excellent men's ward, lofty roomy and well lighted and ventilated by means windows on each side. The want of funds alone prevented this ... but the war, with its list of wounded soldiers served to stimulate the energy of the management, and the generosity of certain charitable donors ... [S]ixteen beds, furnished with complete bedding, etc., were set up, and the Ward was supplied with all the furniture and appliances necessary for the treatment of either medical or surgical cases. Although ample floor area was allowed between and around each of the beds, a considerable space remained empty at the upper end of the room, and this was suitably furnished for the use of convalescents and for the purposes of reading, recreation, etc.

Soldiers enjoying
some refreshments
inside the Buffet.
(Lancashire Record
Office: DDX
2061/1 and Briefing
Media Ltd)

Mayoress Cartmell
and the other
members of the
Buffet Committee,
from *Preston
Guardian*, 4 March
1916. (Preston
Digital Archive and
Briefing Media Ltd)

Further expense was necessarily incurred in the provision of suitable and sufficient bath and lavatory accommodation, which was erected with a due regard to modern hygiene requirements ... The approximate total cost per bed was about £5, and the Hospital, and the town generally, are indebted to the generous donors who contributed to their provision, and a list of these contributions appear at the end of this report.

As soon as ever the fitting up of the Ward had been completed, about 29th October, a contingent of 12 wounded Belgian soldiers was transferred from the Fazackerley Hospital, Liverpool. Naturally the care and treatment of a number of cases such as these implied a considerable increase of work for the nursing sisters and the medical staff ... Most of the patients were suffering from wounds inflicted by shell-fire, and in the course of their treatment a number of operations varying in extent and magnitude were required. The results were satisfactory, and by the end of the year many of the cases were approaching convalescence.

Great interest was taken in the wounded soldiers by subscribers and persons interested in the work of the Hospital, and the management has gratefully to acknowledge many gifts of clothing, boots, etc., of which the men, when able to leave their beds, as a rule stood sorely in need. Great kindness was also extended to them by the provision of motor-car drives [to Greyfriars courtesy of Mr and Mrs Hollins], and free admission to [Preston North End] football matches and entertainments of various kinds.

(DDX 1708/3/21, pp. 2–3)

Other notable examples include special arrangements on tramcars, musical instruments, newspapers, and fruit. Boots and clothes for the Belgian soldiers were donated by many key local figures: Miss Toulmin, the Lady Mayoress, Sir George Toulmin, Sir Frank Hollins, Miss Hollins and many more. (pp. 12–13).

* * *

A letter dated 9 July 1916 was sent to Phyliss Ord, who was away on holiday, from her sister, in Barton. The letter contained details of local events and showed that, despite the war being well under away, some people were not all that concerned.

Dearest Phil,

Mary and I went to the fête yesterday afternoon, with Babbie. The weather was of course too cold for dresses, we had go in our shabby costumes. Babbie turned up in a bran[d] new costume, looking an awful dog. She didn't half know it either … She practically insisted on us going round the hospital with her, said she had left a dirty cap there, which she must fetch. When we did go, she never got the cap at all, that was merely an excuse, she wanted to show herself off to the tommies in her new rig-out.

Mary and I were very keen to see the boxing champion as Billy Wells the champion of England was boxing the ex-champion of Scotland. Babbie, however was not keen, so we refrained from going. One of the tea-stalls was run by the aristocrats of Garstang … They all wore violet-coloured overalls and black hats with a bunch of violets in the front. They certainly looked rather nice …

We retired from the field at about 4.30, being by that time thoroughly bored, not having seen a thing. We went and had tea at the Ribblesdale Cafe, and went to the Palladium to see *The Climax* with Lilian Braithwaite, on the pictures. They were jolly good …

Madam Mivriel has some awfully sweet hats in the window, but I was horribly sick to see that she had actually got another one practically similar to mine. The same sort of ribbon with the big bow behind, and the piece going underneath, and the only difference is that the ribbon goes a wee bit over the crown on one side, and the grapes are red instead of heliotrope, and different coloured flowers of courses, but the effect is the same. It has the black underneath too.

I went yesterday to show it Mary and discovered it had gone. When I was in the cafe at night with Mr Booth and Mary, I actually saw Freda Bowen of all people, going along with it on. I believe she saw mine on the bed, that Sunday, she and Mrs Bowen walked out. The worst of it is, I have never worn mine in Preston yet, and people will think I have copied her …

Heaps of love too Mother and yourself. Hilda.

A contemporary recalled that cinema was put on during the war: 'During the war we went one night in the holiday week. They used to put bits of things on the park and we would go. There was a big crowd of us, my family, my sister's family and friends from across ... It was Bette Davis!'[4] In a further letter, dated 11 April 1916, Phyliss Ord recalled, 'I quite enjoy my walk down to the post every night, you can think of me between 8 and 8 [.30] pm. trolling down to the station.'

* * *

'During the First World War at either side of Plum Pudding Hill the land was let of in plots for people to grow vegetables.' This was part of the work of the Ministry of Food Control, which was created in 1916. In January 1917, the Park and Baths Committee placed at the disposal of the Allotment Committee portions of Moor and Haslam Parks, as they were considered desirable for the purposes of allotments. It was also desired that the land be laid out in model plots (CBP/31/8). On 7 March 1918, there was reported to be opposition to seeding areas of Haslam Park (p. 421). Other national schemes were designed to help raise money for the war effort, particularly war bonds. The council invested £45,000 into war bonds, £40,000 of which was invested on the visit of the 'Tank' to Preston on 21 January 1918 (CBP 28/9, p. 76). A contemporary recalls, 'At the end of the war a big tank came to Preston and my sister and one of the overseers were selling war bonds from this tank and they went to Blackburn and did the same.'[5] A second recalls, 'There was a tank came and it was collecting money and we decided we would go in our breakfast half hour and we were late coming back. The manager asked us where we had been and we told him we had been to see the tank. It was something then to see a tank, you know. It was on the market square.'[6]

A further example of such a scheme was the 'Autumn campaign' organised by the National Free Church Council in 1917. It had five definite objectives, including a focus on home visits to reach out to dependants and widows of servicemen. Another focus was on dealing with the issues of those returning from the war, especially those discharged and wounded, along with the formation of 'working groups' in churches for making knitted comforts for the troops (FCPR 4/1). Such a scheme was in place at Christ church – its May 1917 newsletter reported that 'forty-two pairs of socks and six scarves were sent by our Working-Party to the Town Hall'. A thank you was received from the mayoress, who commented that they were to be sent as a larger order to the 6th Battalion Loyal North Lancashire in Mesopotamia. The newsletter also commented that contributions to the Wool Fund were being placed in Bow Lane Post Office (PR 2952 4/10). A contemporary remembered that his mother encouraged the children to knit socks for soldiers.[7]

A contemporary recalled,

> Other things I remember are when soldiers came home on leave. Their friends in the money used to take them out drinking and when merry with drink, it was not uncommon for some of them to throw handfuls of half-pennies to children just for fun to see them scramble to get some. First they said swear words often coupled with the Kaiser's

Mayoress Cartmell and other ladies posing with their parcels. (Lancashire Lantern: 4949)

name. My sisters and self did not too well on these occasions because, a) we would not scramble, b) it was rude to swear. I have however said a quiet 'bugger' out if my sister's hearing for a penny … Other highlights were fights in the streets which we watched from our window. These were often among women. Maybe it was because their men were away.[8]

A second contemporary adds,

My eldest brother came back from the war, he went at seventeen and the other brother at fifteen, and he came back on leave and my dad had my mother in a corner facing the door, kicking her and he just lifted his rifle up to shoot him and he were only seventeen. Our Nellie came in and knocked him flying from the women's room door [in the Park Hotel]. She said, 'Don't, Mark, it's not worth it.' He said, to him, 'If you lay another finger on my mother, I'll kill you dead and don't ever forget it.' He never hit her any more after that.[9]

***

Politically, the beginning of the war saw much activism from the local unions, mainly on the subject of wages as the impact of the war had made the cost of living higher, much like today's recession, which has seen a constant rise in bills, food prices and rents. It was proposed by unions to the Finance Committee, which in turn passed on its recommendations to the borough council. On 15 December 1915 unions proposed to the Finance Committee, which in turn passed on its recommendations to the borough council, a 'war bonus be granted to continue in force for the duration of the war to Corporation Officials and Employees' (CBP 28/8, p. 354).

The idea was initially refused, in April 1915:

> In view of the regularity and continuity of Employment in the Corporation service and the present rate of Wages and conditions of employment and also to the fact that the Rates of pay have been so recently revised the Sub-Committee cannot recommend any increase in Wages or a War Bonus.
>
> (CBP 28/8, p. 295)

By January 1916, the employees of all the committees that made up the council were receiving a war bonus, from those in the Harris Museum (£2 6s 0d) to the general markets (18s), even those working on the streets and buildings (£37 16s 7d). Initially they were paid for two weeks, with an increase to four-week payments (CBP 20/38, pp. 217–220). The reason for the differing amounts paid among the council committees related to the types of jobs for which each was responsible. There was also an official scale of what bonus employees should receive based on their pay, something that was suggested by the Finance Committee in its review:

War Bonus

> 1. Where the wages do not exceed 30/- a week.   1/- per week
> 2. Where the wages exceed 20/- a week but do not exceed 30/- per week. 2/- per week
> 3. Where the wages exceed 30/- a week but do not exceed 35/- per week. 1/6 per week
> 4. Where the wages exceed 35/- a week but do not exceed 40/- per week. 1/- per week'
>
> (CBP 28/8, p. 354)

* * *

At the same time, the council was still paying an allowance to dependants of employees who were away on active duty; although it seems to have been renamed 'War Service Allowance'. However, following the proposal being passed by the Finance Committee on 12 August 1914, several additions were made (CBP 28/8, p. 242). A motion was passed at a meeting of the Finance Committee, held at the Town Hall on 17 November 1915, summarising all the changes:

> The conditions set forth in the Resolution confirmed by the Council on the 31st December, 1914, with regard to the enlistment of Corporation Officials and Employees, shall only apply to Officials and Employees now eligible for enlistment, who enlist before the 4th December, 1915, under Lord Derby's Scheme or, with consent of the Heads of Department, for immediate service with the Colours, unless before that date they have been rejected by the Military Authorities.
>
> (CBP 28/8, p. 345)

Large food stocks were needed to feed a nation at war. (Lancashire Lantern: 4950)

The deadline for enlistment in the Derby Grouping Scheme was 4 December. The rejection referred to had to come from either the military tribunals or doctors at the recruitment offices.

* * *

In August 1914, as mentioned in chapter 2, the council decided to support those employees who had decided to enlist by offering them reinstatement into their former positions, as well as supporting them with a 'war allowance' of 5s a week. It was later decided that the wages of married men should be altered in line with government guidelines – meaning that the allowance to dependants should continue even if an employee is killed on active service – and that these changes would only apply to those individuals who enlisted before 1 November 1914 and received permission to do so from their heads of department. This date, if the reader recalls, was around the time Preston's recruitment 'boom' was ending, so the idea of having a deadline could have been the council's way of encouraging enlistment. Similar thinking was seen in the motion quoted above, as it contained the deadline of 4 December 1915; this was the final deadline for enlistment under the Derby Scheme. This certainly shows that the council was patriotic, and I think it equally demonstrates that the council were not in favour of supporting anyone that did not feel compelled to do their duty for king and country. However, the decision could also have been financially motivated as the council was short on money, trying to cut costs in September 1915 (CBP 28/8, p. 326).

* * *

Preston's political situation was not limited to Preston Town Council, as local workers were themselves struggling with the increasing cost of living during the First World War. Similar to the experiences discussed above, local unions were in discussion with employers to obtain an increase in pay. The strategy used, however, was to strike. With constant mill closures and the uncertainty of wages, the situation was completely different to that experienced by council employees. A particular problem for the cotton industry was the loss of workforce, as they were either enlisting voluntarily or bring called up without thought for the consequences. Mayor Cartmell explains, 'It was not until many of the men had joined the Army and trade had been seriously injured that some attempt was made to rectify this error' (p. 69). Cartmell was referring to the cotton industry being given protection status under Lord Derby's Scheme.

* * *

Life at home was easy for many Prestonians, and one contemporary recalls that this may have manifested itself into a hatred for Germans:

> There was a lot of ill feeling probably more ill feeling against the Germans in the First World War than in the second. There was one firm had a shop in Avenham Lane and they sold ducks and rabbits and such like. He had a stall in the market and they had a saying, 'Rabbits, fine rabbits and ruddy big ducks.' However, he went out during the First World War. I remember his windows were broken and so on and he vanished. I know of another case of a friend of mine, her parents had a house to let and it was let to a person with German connections and when the war started she was asked, was she going to throw them out? She said, 'No, they were good tenants and paid the rent,' and so forth and they were no trouble to anybody and moved on.[10]

* * *

The legacy of a loved one's death would have been hard to come to terms with. 'When the 1914 War come, four in a family in the Army were nothing. Quite a few families had three or four lads that went. Some went as early as sixteen, seventeen, eighteen and that. So you could have a few [sons] between sixteen and twenty-three that could be in the Army.'[11] However, those that died in the war were not always young. 'He [grandfather] joined up as war was declared. He had been to watch a rugby match and had gone off and that was it. We only saw him once, he had one forty-eight hours' leave and then he went to France and was killed in 1915.'[12] Those that served and killed were not always single. 'He said, "Next time I come home we are getting married

A tank driving down a busy Preston street in order to raise money and awareness for War Bonds.
(Lancashire Lantern: 4966)

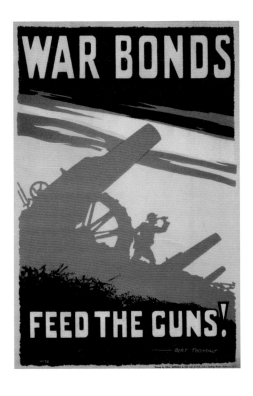

and don't forget!" So we did … that was the end of him as I never saw him no more …
I was only married for four days.'[13] Those that served and killed were also brothers,
fathers and cousins. 'My aunt … used to tell me some glorious stories because they had
lost their son in the 1914 War and that really upset her.'[14] 'My eldest brother was killed
in the First World War, he was twenty-one, he was the oldest. He was only in France for
about three weeks when he was killed.'[15] 'I have eight brothers and one sister … Two
were killed in the First World War.'[16]

* * *

A poem was written anonymously in the *Preston Herald* on 2 September 1914, rather
early in the war, and captures the feelings of those who lost someone in the war:

> To The Loved Ones Of the Fallen. -
> Come Unto Me – and I will Give you Rest.-
> Heart-broken ones! What comfort can we give you,
> What may we do to ease your grief and pain?
> Have fathers gone, or husbands, sons, or brothers,
> Snatch'd from you rudely by the leaden rain?
> Heart-broken ones! 'Tis little we can give you.
> Words die unspoken as we see your grief.
> Love knows no balm but actions good and simple,
> Trusts only God and prays Him send relief.
> Heart-broken ones! There's One whose heart was broken!
> Beneath His robe that heart your sorrow shares;
> His words can sooth whilst ours may find a purpose,
> As they translated merge into prayers.

6

COMING HOME

I had a bet with Mary of 2/6 that the War would be over by Christmas. 25th [1916].[1]

The war ended at 11 a.m. on Monday 11 November 1918 with as much passion as it had started with, and the headlines of local newspapers certainly shared this passion. The *Preston Herald* printed on 16 November 1918, 'ARMISTICE CONCLUDED … NO LOOPHOLE OF ESCAPE.' The *Lancashire Daily Post* was far simpler in its 11 November 1918 issue, but it was still bold and eye-catching: 'GERMANY SIGNS ARMISTICE. TERMS ACCEPTED. ARMSITICE SIGNED AT 5 O'CLOCK THIS MORNING.' On 16 November 1916, the *Preston Guardian*, however, did not declare the end of the war with any sort of headline, except for its small editorial header, 'THE WEEK OF VICTORY.' The report adds, 'We have come to the close of a week that none of us will forget, as it is the week of victory.' Harry Cartmell wrote of his own personal excitement:

> The result [of the Armistice signing] was awaited in Preston with tense excitement … and [with it falling on a Monday, the previous day] 'Mayor's Sunday' was spent in a state of breathless suspense, and it seemed necessary for one who might be called upon at any moment to make some sort of public announcement to keep in touch with the Town Hall and the newspaper offices during the whole of the day.
>
> (pp. 203–204)

He adds of the wider excitement that

> the news came at last on the morning of Monday. A special message was handed to me at half-past ten. By a lucky coincidence that was the time fixed for the presentation of Military Medals on the Town Hall steps … On this occasion there was a greater muster than usual, owing probably to a feeling that something exceptionally interesting might be on foot … [The presentation took place at 10.45 a.m. and a speech followed.] 'I have to announce that the Armistice was signed at five o'clock (at this moment the great bell in the tower began to boom) … ' It was a dramatic moment. The crowd in the Market Place, now grown to several thousands, broke out into tremendous cheering. The cheers

Top: 'Profitable Patriotism' – a take on 'Proud Preston'. (Lancashire Lantern: 4967)

Middle: Celebrating Christmas in 1916, wounded soldiers helping to decorate a tree, from *Preston Guardian*, 30 December 1916. (Courtesy of Briefing Media Ltd)

Bottom: Christmas decorations on the wards. *Preston Guardian*, December 30th 1916. (Courtesy of Briefing Media Ltd)

had hardly died away when the good news was communicated to the town by 'hooters' in the mills, for some time held in readiness. The noise was what would be called [*sic*] cacophanous, but music was never so sweet. The Church bells would ring again and again in due course ... flags ... appeared everywhere as if by magic. The streets were densely thronged by cheering crowds. Workmen marched in procession from all parts of the town. From the early afternoon until late at night band performances were given in the square. At three o'clock when the whole square was filled by a densely packed multitude an attempt was made to give concentration and direction to the shouting. Cheers for the King were followed by the National Anthem ... But though, here and there, spaces, all too small, were cleared for a few of the gayer spirits where the music suggested dancing, and also where it didn't – the behaviour of the people struck many of us as really subdued. There was an entire absence of anything suggesting mafficking. One observed more than a touch of seriousness and was not surprised to learn that, even where such a thing might least have been expected, there was a feeling that the most appropriate celebration could be made in another way. Everywhere it was reported that improvised services were well attended ... [and] the Churches were filled throughout the day by a succession of worshippers.

(p. 204–206)

War Charities Fête, from *Preston Guardian*, 9 September 1916. (Courtesy of Briefing Media Ltd)

The celebrations at the Moor Park Hospital were just as exciting, as Nurse de Trafford proved:

> Great excitement is astir! Will this armistice be signed? It is only a matter of a few days (if it comes off) – before we have peace! Too good to be true – November 10th – A day I shall never forget! – one arrived in the ward saying – 'Armistice signed at 5 a.m. – all hostilities cease at 11 a.m.' – a big cheer from D [ward] boys and nurses standing near at the time – then a minute or two to realise it – then I think we went mad, or a near approach to it!
>
> Off we went to the kit stores – tore open the old Christmas decoration boxes – cut off small Union Jacks which we pinned on our aprons and caps – Matron draped in a garland of red, white and blue paper – which I pinned up for her. Woodfin came and pinned a Union Jack on me – and we three and several nurses started a procession – headed by Quick (orderly) with his mop on high and he was followed by the band, that is a patient clapping two trays together making a most infernal noise – away we went all through the hospital. The procession getting larger and larger as we went – as other ward nurses tacked on to us – the old Matron was quite a sport. 'How do you think I'm to keep the men in order?' She laughed good naturedly though and quite entered into the fun of the day.
>
> All this time mill hooters and bells – went screaming away, and we went outside and listened and could hardly make ourselves believe we had peace at last – thirty days allowed [for the Germans] to decide is the condition – very stiff conditions too – to clear out of Belgium and France, give up all prisoners, 5,000 guns, 1,000 aeroplanes, and goodness knows what else. So at Christmas time (six weeks' time off) we ought to hear of real peace.
>
> (p. 132)

The hospital wasn't the only place affected by the celebrations, as Arthur Procter Cartmell wrote in his business diary:

> News received this day [Monday, 11 November 1918] at 11. a.m. that an Armistice has been signed by Germany for a cessation of hostilities.
>
> To commemorate the event our works [at Cartmell and Sons] were closed at 12 noon until the following Wednesday morning.
>
> Workpeople were not paid their wages for this holiday.
>
> (DDX 1223/3)

* * *

News of the Armistice was also received on the front line and the activities there were equally exciting. Colonel Potter recalled,

> I was the first person he met when he got out, and without a smile of any sort on his face, he said, 'Potter you have an hour and twenty minutes more to fight' … [as] hostilities would cease at 11 a.m … On hearing the war was going to cease, my first feeling was one of disappointment that we were being literally whipped off our quarry just when we

were going to kill, and I still think that it would have been possible as far as we personally were concerned, to have gone on for several days longer ... My second thought was one of thankfulness that no more of my men would be killed ... The news of the armistice had reached the troops and I met a widely cheering mob. I stopped at the head of the column, and presently received a message that the men would like me to ride down the column. I had not made up my mind whether I was glad it was all over, but the men appeared so pleased that I could not help smiling at them. Suddenly one of them shouted out, 'Three cheers for the chap that wants to go on fighting,' and they broke ranks and surrounded me, cheering wildly. I made my way slowly down, but I must confess that I could not speak and that I had tears in my eyes. At two minutes to eleven a shell, the last, came, but did no harm, the last bit of futile spite.

(pp. 154–155)

* * *

Those that made it home from the war still continued to suffer physically. 'I couldn't move [my arm] but could move my hand.'[2] This contemporary suffered injuries to his right arm on the Somme but managed to survive the war and regain employment. A different contemporary remembered how 'my youngest brother died a fortnight after his discharge from the Army as being medically unfit. He was out in the worst of the fighting in the early days of the war and was wet through week after week and it affected his throat – consumption of the throat.'[3] This, however, was not the case for everyone. 'My brother [wasn't killed] ... he was gassed in France, going over the top and they brought him home to Felixstowe and he was in hospital there. Then he was sent home but he managed to regain his sight ... [and later] went into the mill after the war.'[4] A third contemporary recalled, 'In 1914 my father was called into the Coldstream Guards ... [he] was wounded in France and was brought back to England after the war years.'[5]

Returning soldiers also suffered from the psychological effects of war: 'In fact, one of my colleagues at the office, he came back and he was in the 1917–1918 winter. When he came out of the trenches, they had to cut his boots and the clothes off him because they couldn't get them off. They had to cut them off him to let him have a bath. He had been in it so long. It affected him ... he went on to drink.'[6]

Nurse Trafford wrote in May 1919 that 'we've a lot of shell shock ... cases' (p. 140). Of one particular incident she went into some detail:

I had a terrible time with a lunatic – poor wretched chap – he'd most dirty ways – I can never describe what it was like looking after him. He just wallowed in filth and one night we had to change his bedclothes about five times, it nearly made one sick, and I can stand a good lot – not easily put off – he used to get mucked up from his bandaged leg splint to his fingertips – and also used to rake one foot against the bad leg and in doing this he loosened the bandage and dressing – most awful language he used! and pulled such grimaces! – poor unhappy fellow! We had a bank clerk doing orderly one evening and he and I had a really bad time with him. He came to me and (though highly amused) he said in a solemn voice – 'That chap is throwing wool and filth about the room.' 'Oh,' I laughed, 'be prepared for that, he's always in that state!' 'Oh,' he replied, 'as long as we know!' He got so rough we had to get a folded sheet under him, round his body and tie him to the bed, bringing the end of the sheet under the mattress and safety pinning it down on the other side of the bed. Neither the clerk or I will ever forget that chap!

We laughed a great deal – and the fact of our loony behaving was in those ways (disgusting though it was!) got too much for us, and we just had fits of giggling – couldn't help it! We'd get him changed and clean and then he'd say, 'Nurse, you're alright with him now – and keep an eye on the joker and I'll be back again in no time.'

Off he'd go to get a bit of supper or something – and I was left to the loony and his grimaces – he'd a bad self-inflicted wound, poor beggar – which had to be dressed – he'd a trick of pulling up the bedclothes tight over his face and tucking them under his head and he'd lie like a man in a coffin. He was always and forever asking for a chocolate. 'Nurse, have you got a chocolate.' One night he bothered us so, that we raided some man's locker in the 'tents' and found some – he plucked them out of our hands and stuffed them into his mouth and immediately inquired, 'Nurse, have you got a chocolate?' It was the same question – till one was sick and tired of having him. We couldn't manage him – he was taken off by ambulance to Winnick Asylum, a nice handful for someone to look after if he continued in his ways!

(pp. 110–111)

* * *

The lasting effect of the war varied between people. One contemporary, for example, who was very attached to her wartime letters, commented, 'It's not very long ago that I burned all his [her husband's] letters from France. Because I thought they are not for anybody to read. And I saved them all those years and I couldn't see to read them so well so I burned them.'[7] A second recalled, somewhat more generally, 'I think the majority, the 1914 War, people come to be more isolated. Before that, nobody decorated their home. After the 1914 War it started, these young lads come back from soldiering and they have bought paper, I have bought paper as low as 4 1/2d a roll, and they were more house-proud.'[8] Similar changes were seen in other directions: 'When [my brother] came out of the Army he went down on a farm and he enjoyed the outdoor life ... I think a lot of soldiers in the First World War wanted to go outside when they came back. I have heard this from a lot of people. They wouldn't go back inside again.'[9]

There were, however, more positives experiences of the war that offered a lasting legacy:

As a child I always had a liking for animals other than dogs, horses and chicken being my favourites. In a field, now part of Deepdale and Blackpool Road, I had seen a horse and foal. I decided to have the foal. One day I took a length of string in my pocket, climbed the spike gate and approached the foal. I did not get very near however before the mother came to look at me and I fled. In climbing over the gate I got stuck on the spikes. There I was, screaming my head off and the mother horse smelling at me. I was lifted off by a passing soldier, none the worse. It dawned on me later that I should not steal.[10]

* * *

In the short term the effects of the end of the war were quite clear. Mayor Cartmell wrote that

> everyone realised that many of the abnormal regulations proper to a state of War must necessarily continue in force. There was little hope of any relaxation of the rather irksome food restrictions, though the white bread which made its appearance almost immediately was accepted as a welcome instalment. The new freedom from aircraft peril was indicated by the withdrawal of the lighting restrictions. It was like meeting an old friend to see the lighted dial of the Town Hall clock, and to hear the loud notes of the great bell which had been so long silent at night. In the streets there was sufficient illumination to prevent accidents, but no more than that as the need for coal economy remained. The state of Armistice made little change in some of our War Institutions. The Sailors' and Soldiers' Buffet at the Railway Station, the Hostels at Ashton and in Fishergate, the Hospital at Moor Park, continued their operations, for soldiers would continue to travel for many a long month yet, and, though the tale of the wounded was closed, there were many still to be nursed.
>
> (p. 207)

Of the closing of the Moor Park Hospital, Nurse de Trafford wrote,

> The committee have behaved vilely lately, in such an underhand way. They arrange things without consisting Matron, they even waited till she was away on a few day's holiday, to hold a meeting to decide on closing the hospital – on the grounds that 'the V[oluntary] A[ided] D[etachment]s were tired,' and that 'funds were wanted'. Matron being one of the committee, it was odd to arrange this without her being present. We VADs were up in arms, naturally, about being 'Tired' – as not single girl wished to leave and we are all devoted to the place and our work.
>
> As for the funds – we have £2,500 in the bank at the present time and as the government pay two-thirds of the upkeep of the hospital, that sum would last us several months more without appealing for further money from the Preston people. The hospital is well staffed and everything is running so smoothly and well, it seems a shame to shut down the place, especially now – as men from distant hospitals are allowed transfers quite easily (they used to be very hard to get).
>
> Now if the place is closed, Preston boys will have nowhere to go except the 'Fulwood Military' or 'Whalley' where there are no comforts such as a VAD one can give them – and all this money has been collected and given by Preston people – so that it seems hard if their own boys are not to benefit by it. We are Whalley's biggest VAD, and we are a primary hospital. Very few VADs have had trains of wounded from France as we've done … The old committee are just tired I suppose and want to shake themselves clear of the job – but they've not acted in the right way. Men from the hospital, outsiders, VADs and unknown writers, have written long letters in the *Lancashire Daily Post* – protesting strongly against the closing and the way the committee are going on.

We are to close February 1st [1919] – unless things can be altered, which I hope and pray may be!

(pp. 133–134)

Cartmell continues:

But some great and significant changes took place at once [following the Armistice]. The Tribunal met on the 13th, transacted certain formal business, and adjourned *sine die;* all the members being conscious that they would never again be called upon to exercise their functions. The activities of the Prisoners of War Aid Society [also] came suddenly to an end; for parcels which took four or five weeks to reach their destination would be of no use to men whose almost immediate release was expected. Belgian Refugees had received notices anticipating the result of the Armistice by four or five weeks. It remained only to take formal leave of them. One institution disappeared a little later, and no tears were shed. The people who carried on the work of National Service, a new name for the old 'Military Service', in the premises of the Conservative Club in Guildhall Street, a business which employed at one time 320 persons, found their occupation gone when no more soldiers were to be pressed in. They therefore closed down just before Christmas [1918?], the greater number of the assistants being transferred to the Army Pay Office, a department whose activities were expected to become greater for some time.

* * *

The end of the war meant that those men who were serving would be able to come home, although many had to wait to be demobilised. It also meant that the regimental colours of those regiments could be returned, none more anticipated than the long-awaited sequel to the handing over of the colours of the 1st Battalion Loyal North Lancashire Regiment on 5 August 1914. Mayor Cartmell had huge expectations, but they were to be dashed:

I had pictured a great and enthusiastic welcome to our home-coming troops with every circumstance of pomp and dignity, in which the ceremonial restoration of the Regimental Colours, long laid up in the Town Hall, would be the crowning symbol of victory. It was with feeling akin to disappointment that I received a telegram from the Commanding Officer of the 1st Battalion of the Loyal North Lancashire, dispatched shortly after the signing of the Armistice, intimidating that it was desired that the Colours should be sent over-seas as early as possible. The Colour party arrived within a few days, and, in consequence of delay arising from some hesitation on the part of the War Office in sanctioning the proposal, the arrangements had to be made at very short notice. Nevertheless in the function which took place on the 26th November [1918], I think we succeeded in imparting something of dignity to the proceedings all too brief. In spite of very dull and threatening weather a great concourse, half filling the Square, had gathered to witness the proceedings. The Colour party … had come direct from France for the purpose. There was an escort from the Barracks with buglers, and the band of the King's Own Royal Lancaster Regiment was in attendance. For my own part I tried to say things appropriate to the occasion … And the buglers sounded appropriate calls the band played the National Anthem which was followed by cheers for the King and for the first Battalion. The Party then taking possession of the Colours proceeded to join their escort, and, with the band playing, marched along Fishergate to the Station ... A newspaper writer [wrote] ... 'No event in Alderman Cartmell's Mayoralty has given him greater satisfaction or is likely to live longer in his recollection than this morning's ceremony.'

(pp. 208–209)

This event was quickly followed by the return of the 4th Battalion – the Territorials ... on Friday the 6th December.

(p. 210)

* * *

A further ceremony took place to mark 'another war chapter' on 28 January 1919, with more than 650 repatriated prisoners of war from the Loyal North Lancashire Regiment returning to Preston. They assembled at the town hall on the invitation of the Committee of the Prisoners of War Help Society. Mayor Cartmell continues:

It was remarked that they were a happy looking and jovial crowd, betraying nothing in their manner or their physical appearance of the privations endured in their prison camps. It was with much eagerness and vigour that they shook hands with the Mayoress and Mrs Cuthbert Pyke, who as President and Secretary of the Committee received them at the top of the stairs. They then passed into the Guildhall which was decorated in their honour with many conservatory plants and hung with flags of the Allies and the Red Cross Society ... A concert had been arranged but there was a necessary interval for the preparation of the Hall and this they spent in the room of the P.S.A. close by, when in the breathing spaces of an improvised sing-song, they had an opportunity of exchanging notes on their adventures. When the men re-assembled at the Guildhall there was a little speech-making before the evening's entertainment began, and some attempt was made to give expression to the gladness of our rejoicing at seeing face-to-face those who had occupied so much of our thought during three-and-a-half anxious years ... After the repatriated Prisoners of War the survivors of the first Expeditionary Force and the nearest relatives of those who fell in the Great Retreat to receive the Mons Star, the most prized of service medals. The men, mostly from the Loyal North Lancashire Regiment (1st Batt.) who assembled in the Guildhall on the 22nd February, 1919, numbered nearly 200, the relatives of those killed 70. The demeanour of the audience was altogether different from anything I have experienced before or since. They listened to the story, as I tried to recount it, with the gravest attention, taking up the points with expressive interjections of assent ... Those who witnessed this impressive function will never forget the emotion displayed by the widows present as I ventured to say a few words of comfort before handing to them the medals bearing the names of the men whose loss they mourned. I look back on this as the most trying of all my experiences.

(pp. 212–214)

* * *

'A Preston VC died a short time ago – he was not at this hospital – but he came to see the men one day – his bottom jaw had been shot away – he was getting on well, but had a third operation and died under anaesthetic, poor fellow.' Nurse de Trafford continues: 'Our men collected £2. 6s amongst themselves – for a wreath – a huge red, white and blue anchor – a glorious one – they are so nice towards one another – and are as gentle and helping as any woman – to their fellow wounded' (p. 6). The Victoria Cross holder she is referring to is Private Young. Mayor Cartmell explains the wider significance of the man:

> The town was thrown into a state of excitement on the occasion of the official reception of Private Young of the East Lancashire Regiment, the first and only soldier connected with Preston to gain the Victoria Cross. His progress along Fishergate to the Town Hall, preceded by a band playing 'See the Conquering Hero Comes', was a great triumph, and the official welcome accorded to him in the Market Square was witnessed by a great and enthusiastic multitude, amongst those who joined in the plaudits being seven of his nine young children, who were awaiting him on the balcony of the Town Hall. The official proceedings ended, the hero of the day, accompanied by his wife and young children, was driven by a devious route through a cheering throng to his home in Heysham Street, a home hardly recognisable owing to the transformation that friendly hands had effected there.
>
> Three months later the town paid a second and final tribute to Private Young, V.C. He never recovered from his terrible wounds, and died under the treatment in hospital. The military funeral was probably the most impressive ever witnessed in Preston.
>
> (pp. 106–107)

Mayor Cartmell adds a rather poignant tribute to him: 'Private Young, V.C, found a last resting place amongst his own people, and in that respect his case is exceptional. Most of those who have been killed rest where they fell, many in nameless graves' (p. 107). It is also worth mentioning that in his *For Remembrance*, the mayor lists the subscriptions up to June 1919 of Preston's war charity funds. With this were the totals raised from the presentation (£561 11s 8d) and memorial (£47 16s 0d) of Private Young (p. 135–136).

* * *

Arthur Procter Cartmell wrote on 11 November 1918, 'At this time an epidemic of "Flu" is raging in the town and our coffin maker could not have a holiday and was paid double for this.' A contemporary also commented, 'I didn't realise it [the Flu epidemic] was history because I didn't realise it was serious. I knew people were dropping dead all over the place. You wondered who was going to be next.'[11]

POSTSCRIPT

In order that no name be forgotten and that entries be kept up to date, forms have been printed which may be had at the Harris Free Library and it is hoped that relatives make application for them and fill them up.[1]

A contemporary reflecting on the war commented, 'We had gone through such a lot in the First World War.'[2] Rudolf Ord claimed in 1919 that 'hatred for the English was poured into the Germans by mouthfuls long before the war began'. Harry Cartmell wrote in November 1918 that Preston 'would erect a memorial ... expressing gratitude for its soldiers' sacrifice'. 'The town did,' states John Garlington, 'after a drawn-out and tortuous process which lasted ten years. Unfortunately, Sir Harry never saw it or the roll of honour, which would have been a fitting end to his wartime work' (p. 2). The *Preston Guardian* printed his obituary. On 12 May 1923 it commented, 'Sir Harry was an advocate for a war memorial upon the centre of the flagged market.' Cartmell died in May 1923 at his Goosnargh residence after a period of ill health and after recently returning from a trip to France for medical reasons. It is unfortunate he was not able to see through his proposed memorial idea, but his passion and commitment to the people of Preston during the hardships brought about by the war are what should be remembered; the *Preston Guardian* adds that 'during the raising of the forces, Sir Harry acted as chairman of the local tribunal. Saturday after Saturday, too, his was a familiar figure on the occasions of the presentations of military medals and other decorations to Preston soldiers.'

* * *

Returning the Colours of the
1st Battalion Loyal North
Lancashire Regiment – December
1918. (Lancashire Lantern: 4964)

Returning the colours of the
4th (Territorial) Battalion Loyal
North Lancashire Regiment – 12
June 1919 (Lancashire Lantern:
4983)

Farewell band of the 4th
(Territorial) Battalion Loyal
North Lancashire Regiment
(Lancashire Lantern: 4915).

A waiting crowd of spectators watch the Peace Day parade. (Lancashire Lantern: 4984)

Horse-drawn carriages formed part of the Peace Day Parade. (Lancashire Lantern: 4985)

This was a grand occasion, as the magnificent costumes of the children, and the lavishly decorated floats, quite clearly show. (Lancashire Lantern: 4986)

The following was delivered to every house in Preston by Boy Scouts, Girl Guides, and the members of the Crescent Club.

THE MAYOR'S APPEAL

Mayor's Parlour,
Town Hall, Preston,
February 20th, 1924.

To My Fellow Townspeople,

It is the ardent desire of the people of Preston that the long delayed Memorial to the men who gave their lives for their Country should be erected before the next anniversary of the Armistice Day. I beg to inform you that a Committee has been appointed to carry this into effect, and they have decided, after careful consideration, that the Memorial should take the form of a Monument to be erected on a suitable Site, and thereby place on permanent record the tribute of the town to their Noble Sacrifice. I have been requested to open a Mayor's Fund for the purpose of raising the necessary amount.

Arrangements are being made so as to give EVERY MAN, WOMAN, AND CHILD IN PRESTON an opportunity of voluntarily contributing to the Fund.

The names of all Contributors will be inscribed in a book and kept as a record, but without stating the amounts subscribed.

A collector will call upon you during the course of next week, and it is important that you see that your name and address and those of any members of your family who wish to contribute, together with the amounts contributed, are clearly and corrected entered in the Official Collecting Book which is provided for that purpose, and which bears a facsimile of my signature.

I make my Appeal in full confidence of your support.

Yours faithfully,

F.W.F Matthew,

Mayor

* * *

The Right Worshipful The Mayor (Mr Councillor Wooley):

Mindful of the men of this town who suffered unto death in the Great War, and wishing to keep the memory of their great sacrifices ever alive before the eyes of our children's children, we, their fellow-citizens, have erected this Cenotaph; and we ask your Lordship, who know their service, and who have yourself done such great service for the Nation, to unveil it.

Parade of Preston's Citizen
Defence Corps, later
Volunteer Defence Corps.
(Lancashire Lantern: 4970)

Private Young and his
family on the balcony of
the Town Hall. (Lancashire
Lantern: 4956.)

The military procession of
Private Young's funeral.
(Lancashire Lantern: 4958)

These words were delivered as part of the opening ceremony of Preston's war memorial on Sunday 13 June 1926. In the new year work began on the roll of honour, which is located on the stairs of the Harris Museum; it was unveiled on Wednesday 2 November 1927. A third memorial was constructed previous to this at the New Hall Lane Cemetery on 25 May. John Garlington comments that the sword of sacrifice memorial 'came as a surprise for most people as this event was overshadowed by activities surrounding the other monuments'. He adds an interesting statistic: '324 servicemen from World War One who had died in Preston are buried in the cemetery' (p. 11). From my own previous research, at least two were Preston Pals.

* * *

'A Memorial Service to Scouts who have fallen in the war, was held on Sunday March 30th [19]19 in the parish church, and St Mary's church Friargate. A combined parade assembled on the spare land off Lancaster Road for this service. Ten troops were refreshed by 10 officers and 281 scouts.' Altogether, twenty-eight men are recorded as 'Scouts who have Fallen', and four of those that served received the military medal, while another was mentioned in dispatches (DDX 1440/5).

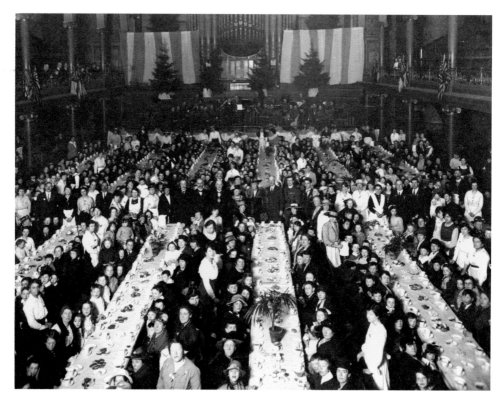

The celebrations extended to a meal for the wives and children of fallen soldiers in the Public Hall. (Lancashire Lantern: 4987)

Portrait of Sir Harry Cartmell by Sir William
Llewellyn. (Courtesy of the Cartmell family)

Portrait of Lady Cartmell by Sir William
Llewellyn. (Courtesy of the Cartmell family)

Both halves of the roll of honour, which is located on the steps of the Harris Museum
and Art Gallery. (Courtesy of Northern Studios)

The unveiling of Preston's largest war memorial by Earl Jellicoe, from *Preston Guardian*, 19 June 1926. (Courtesy of Briefing Media Ltd)

A wider look at the crowd and the military formations bowing their heads from *Preston Guardian*, 19 June 1926. (Courtesy of Briefing Media Ltd)

The number of those in attendance is clear to see. From *Preston Guardian*, 19 June 1926. (Courtesy of Briefing Media Ltd)

NOTES

Introduction

1. Harry Cartmell, *For Remembrance* (1919), p. 275. He was referring to the story of the whole war but I thought it a poignant way to begin the book.
2. 'Table 10 – Administrative Counties, Urban Districts, Rural Districts, &c.', *Census Of England And Wales* (1911), p. 184. This information has been reused under the Open Government License: http://www.nationalarchives.gov.uk/doc/open-government-licence/open-government-licence.htm.

1 Outbreak of War

1. Vicar's Letter', *St Thomas' Parish Newsletter*, 29 August 1914. Lancashire Record Office: PR 3309/14/17.
2. 'Interview with Mr T3P', Elizabeth Roberts Archive, Centre For North West Studies, University of Lancaster, p. 63. Hereafter 'ERC'.
3. ERC, Mrs A2P, p. 6.
4. ERC, Mrs B1P, p. 59.

2 Preparations at Home

1. *St Matthews Magazine*, August 1915.
2. ERC, Mr and Mrs B4P, p. 1.
3. ERC, Mrs W4P, p. 3.
4. ERC, Mr and Mrs B4P, pp. 1 and 8.
5. ERC, Mr B7P, p. 7.
6. ERC, Mr D2P, p. 33.
7. ERC, Mrs A2P, pp. 6 and 29.
8. ERC, Mrs H2P, p. 3.

9. ERC, Mr D3P, p. 14.
10. ERC, Mr and Mrs D2P, p. 34.

3 Work of War

1. ERC, Mr B8P, p. 6.
2. ERC, Mrs A2P, p. 3.
3. ERC, Mr B7P, p. 3.
4. ERC, Mrs A2P, p. 5.
5. ERC, Mr D2P, p. 3.
6. ERC, Mrs B2P, pp. 20–21.
7. ERC, Mrs B4P, p. 29.
8. ERC, Mrs G2P, pp. 5–6.
9. ERC, Mr C1P, p. 16.
10. ERC, Mrs B1P, p. 59.
11. ERC, Mr D1P, p. 47.
12. ERC, Mrs J1P, p. 7.
13. ERC, Mr D2P, p. 33.
14. ERC, Mr and Mrs B4P, p. 13.
15. ERC, S4P, pp. 15, 42 and 16.
16. ERC, Mrs B2P, p. 21.
17. ERC, Mr I1P, p. 5.
18. ERC, Mr F1P, p. 25.
19. ERC, Mr T2P, p. 35.
20. ERC, Mrs S1P, p. 16.
21. ERC, Mr G1P, pp. 75–76.
22. ERC, Mrs P2P, p. 24.
23. ERC, Mr D2P, p. 34.
24. ERC, Mr S6P, p. 2.
25. ERC, Mr C5P, p. 5.
26. ERC, Mr T2P, pp. 34–35.
27. ERC, Mrs W4P, p. 3.
28. ERC, Mrs J1P, p. 1.

4 News from the Front Line

1. 23 August, 1st Battalion Loyal North

Lancashire War Diary, 5 August 1914 – 3 December 1915, Lancashire Infantry Museum.

5 While You're Away

1. 2 April 1916, Rudolf Ord Collection, Lancashire Infantry Museum.
2. ERC, Mr S6P, p. 2.
3. ERC, Mrs D3P, p. 1.
4. ERC, Mrs B1P, p. 67.
5. ERC, Mrs J1P, pp. 1 and 7.
6. ERC, Mrs H2P, pp. 3–4.
7. ERC, Mr B7P, p. 17.
8. ERC, Mr D2P, p. 34.
9. ERC, Mrs H1P, p. 13.
10. ERC, Mr C1P, p. 90.
11. ERC, Mr G1P, p. 68.
12. ERC, Mrs D3P, p. 20.
13. ERC, Mrs C3P, p. 41.
14. ERC, Mr F2P, p. 3.
15. ERC, Mrs O1P, p. 4.
16. ERC, Mr L1P, p. 10.

6 Coming Home

1. 25 December 1916, Rudolf Ord Collection, Lancashire Infantry Museum.
2. ERC, Mr T1P, p. 2.
3. ERC, Mr C1P, p. 32.
4. ERC, Mrs M1P, p. 18.
5. ERC, Mrs C8P, p. 1.
6. ERC, Mr B7P, p. 7.
7. ERC, Mrs C2P, p. 16.
8. ERC, Mr G1P, p. 71.
9. ERC, Mr G2P, p. 17.
10. ERC, Mr D2P, p. 34.
11. ERC, Mr G2P.

Postscript

1. *Preston Guardian*, October 1917, quoted in John Garlington, *A Worthy Monument: The Story of Preston's War Memorial 1917 to 1927* (2006), p. 3.
2. ERC, Mrs P1P, p. 41.

BIBLIOGRAPHY

Primary Sources

Books

Harry Cartmell, *For Remembrance* (Geo Toulmin & Sons, 1919)

Martin Kevill (ed.), *The Personal Diary of Nurse de Trafford 1916–1920* (The Book Guild Ltd, 2001)

War History of the 1st/2nd Battalion (Geo Toulmin & Sons, 1921)

Bound Newsletters

The Hoghtonian, Harris Museum & Art Gallery

Censuses

'Table 13– Occupations (Condensed List) of Males and Females Aged 10 and upwards 1911', Preston, *Census Of England And Wales* (1911), p. 236

'Table 8 – Urban Districts', *Census Of England And Wales* (1911), p. 31.

Church Publications

Christ Church Magazine, September 1914, Lancashire Record Office: PR 2952 4/1

St Matthews' Magazine, Lancashire Record Office: PR 3305/14/3

St Thomas' Newsletter, Lancashire Record Office: PR 3309/14/17

(Note that there is more than one edition of each of these magazines.)

Interviews

Elizabeth Roberts Archive, Centre for North West Studies, University of Lancaster.

Manuscripts

Agriculture Farmers Association Minutes, Lancashire Record Office: DDX 1706/1/4

Arthur Procter Cartmell, Business Diary, Lancashire Record Office: DDX 1223/3

Finance Committee Minutes, 17 May 1911– 16 May 1917, Lancashire Record Office: CBP 28/8 (Note that using the index at the front can help locate specific events.)

Finance Committee Minutes, 24 May 1917– 12 February 1921, Lancashire Record Office: CBP 28/9

Harding Coach Makers Wage Book, Lancashire Record Office: DDX: 460/19

Minutes of the Committee for Relief of Distress and Belgian Refugees Reception Committee, Lancashire Record Office: CBP 53/11

Park and Baths Committee Minutes, 15 February 1909–16 February 1920, Lancashire Record Office: CBP/31/8

Preston and District Boy Scouts Association, Record Book, Lancashire Record Office: DDX 1440/5

Private Wage Book, Horrockses, Lancashire Record Office: DDHS 39

Proceedings of the Lancashire Agricultural War Committee, 2 October 1916–21 October 1919, Lancashire Record Office: CC/WAM 2

Proceedings of the Lancashire Agricultural War Committee, 4 October 1915–29 May 1916, Lancashire Record Office: CC/WAM 1

Signed Council Minutes, 25 March – 26 October 1916, Lancashire Record Office: CBP 20/38

Signed Council Minutes, 25 September 1913

– 25 September 1915, Lancashire Record Office: CBP 20/37

Soldiers and Sailors Buffet Rules, in a scrapbook compiled by Mrs Blackhurst, a Preston suffragette, Lancashire Record Office: DDX 2182/1

War Memorial Subscribers Book, Harris Museum

Paintings

Portraits of Mayor and Mayoress Cartmell by Sir William Llewellyn, Preston Town Hall.

Pamphlets

Annual Report of St Joseph's Hospital (1914), Lancashire Record Office: DDX 1708/3/21

Free Church War Service, Autumn Campaign, Lancashire Record Office: FCPR 4/1

Margaret Wilding, *The War*, Harris Museum & Art Gallery

Sailors' and Soldiers' Free Buffet Information Pamphlet, Lancashire Record Office: DDX 2061/1

The Unveiling of the Preston War Memorial (1926), Harris Museum & Art Gallery

Printed Letters

Lord Derby to Sir George Arthur, 5 July 1915, quoted in Randolph Spencer Churchill, *Lord Derby: King of Lancashire* (Heinemann, 1959), p. 186.

Recollections

Major W. G. Cragg, *With the Loyal North Lancs Regt In Gallipoli and Mesopotamia* (1917), Lancashire Infantry Museum.

Recollections of C. B. Mawbey in 'Middlebrook Somme 1916', Liddle Collection, Special Collections, University of Leeds

Recollections of Col C. K. Potter (55th Division), 1914–1918, Lancashire Infantry Museum

Regimental War Diaries

1st Battalion Loyal North Lancashire War Diary, 5 August 1914–3 December 1915, Lancashire Infantry Museum.

7th Battalion War Diary, Lancashire Infantry Museum.

Unprinted Letters

Ada Whiteside letters, Harris Museum & Art Gallery. There is also a display in the museum.

The letters of Arthur Smith, Captain Duckworth, Rudolf Ord and Sergeant Rawcliffe are located at the Lancashire Infantry Museum.

Secondary Sources

Garraway Ltd, *History of the English Electric Company*, 1951.

Alick Hadwen, 'Roll of Honour of Those Who Died and to Record and Commemorate Those Who Served in the Great War 1914–1918', Online: www.ww1.pgsassociation.org.uk [accessed January 2014]

J. H. Price, *The Dick, Kerr Story* (W. J. Ray & Co. Ltd, 1993).

John Garlington, *A Worthy Monument: The Story of Preston's War Memorial 1917 to 1927* (2006)

TIMELINE OF LOCAL EVENTS

This is a guide only and does not include all the events. It is also only detailed up to January 1916.

1914

28 June: Franz Ferdinand is assassinated.

4 August: Germany invades neutral Belgium. Britain declares war on Germany in response.

5 August: Announcements of the war appear in local newspapers.

11 September: Height and chest measurement requirements are increased and have an immediate effect on recruiting numbers.

12 September: Batches of between 80 and 400 men are sent for voluntary billeting.

19 September: During the 'rush to the colours' it is reported that detachments averaging over 2,000 per day have been sent to the training stations without waiting for uniform.

14 November: An update occurs in the recruitment news after a large absence. It is argued that October was the end of Preston's recruitment 'boom' and here begins the town's decline in recruitment.

27 November: Lord Derby gives a speech at Preston Public Hall.

2 December: Wives and mothers of Preston sailors and soldiers entertained at the public hall.

7 December: Departure of the Preston Pals.

25 December: Troops call an unofficial truce in the trenches.

1915

4 January: Recruitment meeting at Leyland Motors.

3 April: Employers consider use of female labour.

19 May: Lord Derby visits a second time and delivers a speech on the market square as part of a wider drive by the West Lancashire Territorial Association, of which Lord Derby was chairman. Recruitment advertisements to secure men for the territorials and the artillery begin in the newspapers. Recruitment adverts begin for 'Hollins' Company'.

19 June: Lord Derby makes a third speech to the workforce at Messrs J. Foster & Sons, a munition works on Bow Lane.

12 July: A conference takes place between Lord Derby and representatives of Lancashire constituencies at County Hall, Preston. Discussions take place on the Volunteer Corps and other issues.

14 July: The departure of Preston Pals takes place after a three-day leave. Emotional scenes at

the railway station. The mayor walks through each carriage shaking hands.

15 July: The National Registration Act is passed, requiring a census to be undertaken to establish how many men between the ages of fifteen and sixty-five are working and in what trade. It is seen as a step towards stimulating enlistment as voluntary recruitment is not producing the necessary number of recruits.

26 August: A garden fête is held on Avenham and Miller Parks as part of a week-long recruitment drive organised by Lord Derby, known to be his second-best recruiting campaign according to the *Preston Guardian*. He is unable to attend in person but it is attended by thousands. The fête was organised on behalf of the 4th (Territorial) Battalion Loyal North Lancashire.

28 August: It is reported that the week-long drive did not produce a large number of recruits; those who did volunteer were too young.

2 September: Sir George Toulmin speaks at a recruiting meeting at the Goosnargh Show.

8 September: A meeting is held in the town hall to discuss the recruitment situation – the local artillery need fifty men to give them full establishment and the 4th Loyals require at least 800 men to bring the three battalions up to strength.

2 October: A military show takes place on the market square to celebrate recent Allied successes on the Western Front.

9 October: The *Preston Guardian* prints details of a patriotic procession through Preston that is designed to raise funds for the provision of winter comforts for the troops on the front. Crowds line the streets. It also reports that that 'Hollins' Company' has begun a week-long leave period. They visit the harvest thanksgiving service at St Joseph's parish church and leave Preston station to cheering crowds on the platform.

11 October: Lord Derby appointed Director-General of Recruiting.

21 October: Lord Derby announces his recruitment plan after being appointed Director-General of Recruiting. His plan is designed to extend voluntary recruitment by allowing civilians to become more involved and is nicknamed the 'Derby Scheme' after its creator, or 'Grouping Scheme' after its methodology.

6 November: The *Preston Guardian* prints details of the positive response to the Derby Scheme. The work involved in canvassing of all the 'unstarred' men (those not working in industries deemed vital for the war effort) was also severely underestimated; an extension is granted until 11 December.

5 December: In the *Preston Guardian*, canvassers report that the large number of promises to attest do not correspond with the number of actual attestations.

11 December: The final day of voluntary enlistment under the Derby Scheme sees a rush to enlist; strategies are put in place to deal with the situation.

12 December: Lord Derby reports on his recruitment campaign to Lord Kitchener; recruitment figures show that single men are still holding back and that married men, who would be called up last in the groups, are enlisting in larger numbers than single men. Preston's figures corroborate this.

1916

10 January: The first groups of Derby recruits from Preston and Fulwood report for duty.

15 January: The details of three local tribunals established in Preston, each hearing cases from different areas of the region, are printed in the *Preston Guardian*. They are set up to hear applications from individuals, or on behalf of them, for exemption under the Derby Scheme.

27 January: The Military Service Act passes.